MODERN ZEN

Ancient Wisdom for a Balanced and Busy Life

FELIX GRAYSON

MINDSPARK
PUBLISHING

To those seeking balance amidst the chaos and stillness in the noise—may this book guide you to the peace already within you. This is for the dreamers, the seekers, and the mindful souls who walk the path of presence with grace.

"When you realize nothing is lacking, the whole world belongs to you."

— *Lao Tzu*

ABOUT STONED PHILOSOPHER

Welcome to the *Stoned Philosopher* series—where timeless wisdom meets the modern world.

Each book distills powerful lessons from history's greatest minds, leaders, and thinkers—transforming their ideas into practical insights for today's challenges.

From mastering habits, calm, and resilience to understanding success, leadership, and meaning, this collection invites you to think deeper, live wiser, and see life from new perspectives.

Whether you're exploring *Modern Zen*, uncovering *The Wisdom of Warriors*, or seeking clarity through *The Art of Perspective*, every title offers a journey toward self-mastery and understanding.

Discover the full *Stoned Philosopher* collection and more at **FelixGrayson.com**, home of **Mind-Spark Publishing**—where knowledge, philosophy, and storytelling come together to spark lifelong curiosity.

Wisdom isn't something we find—it's something we grow into.

Let the journey begin.

CONTENTS

INTRODUCTION: A JOURNEY INTO THE HEART OF ZEN

The world is moving faster than ever. Our days are filled with endless tasks, distractions, and obligations, leaving us yearning for moments of stillness, clarity, and purpose. In this whirlwind of modern life, how do we find balance? How do we cultivate peace amidst chaos? How do we live with intention rather than simply moving from one moment to the next? The answers lie in a practice as ancient as it is timeless: Zen.

Zen is not a religion, a philosophy, or a set of rules. It is a way of being—an invitation to live with presence, simplicity, and harmony. Rooted in the teachings of ancient masters and yet profoundly relevant to our contemporary challenges, Zen offers practical wisdom for navigating life's complexities with grace and resilience. It calls us to let go of what no longer serves us, to embrace the beauty of impermanence, and to connect deeply with ourselves, others, and the world around us.

This book is your guide to that way of being. It is not a roadmap with rigid instructions but a collection of insights, practices, and reflections to help you discover your own path. Together, we will explore what it means to live a Zen-inspired life—a life rooted in balance, enriched by mindfulness, and guided by timeless principles that transcend the noise of the modern world.

The Call for Balance

At some point, we all feel it—a quiet longing for something more meaningful, more grounded, more authentic. Perhaps it arises in moments of stillness, when the clamor of daily life subsides and we can hear the whisper of our inner selves. Or perhaps it comes during times of struggle, when the weight of stress and busyness becomes too much to bear. This longing is not a sign of weakness; it is an invitation to rediscover what truly matters.

Zen begins with this recognition. It meets us where we are, offering tools to cultivate awareness and presence in our everyday lives. Unlike quick fixes or temporary solutions, Zen provides a foundation for lasting transformation—a way to navigate life's challenges with clarity and purpose. It reminds us that balance is not something we achieve once and for all but something we practice, moment by moment.

The Essence of Zen

Zen's beauty lies in its simplicity. It does not ask us to abandon our responsibilities or retreat from the world. Instead, it invites us to engage with life more fully, seeing each moment as an opportunity for mindfulness, growth, and connection.

At its heart, Zen teaches us to let go of distractions and attachments, to embrace the present moment with openness and curiosity. This practice of presence transforms even the most ordinary experiences—washing dishes, walking to work, sharing a meal—into moments of meditation. It is not about doing more but about being more—more attentive, more compassionate, more aligned with our values.

Zen also reminds us of the interconnectedness

of all things. In the words of Zen master Thích Nhất Hạnh, "We are here to awaken from the illusion of our separateness." This perspective shifts how we see ourselves and the world, fostering a sense of gratitude, humility, and responsibility.

A Modern Approach to an Ancient Practice

While Zen's origins trace back to ancient traditions, its teachings are remarkably relevant to the challenges of modern life. In a world dominated by multitasking, distractions, and constant stimulation, Zen offers a counterbalance—a way to slow down, focus, and reconnect with what is truly important.

This book bridges the wisdom of Zen with the realities of contemporary living. Each chapter explores a different aspect of Zen practice, from cultivating mindfulness and resilience to fostering creativity and building meaningful relationships. You will find practical strategies, inspiring stories, and thoughtful reflections designed to help you integrate Zen into your daily routines.

Whether you are new to Zen or have been practicing for years, this book provides tools and insights to deepen your understanding and apply its principles in meaningful ways. It is a guide not only to mindfulness but to a way of life that is grounded, intentional, and deeply fulfilling.

What You Will Discover

As you journey through these pages, you will explore themes that resonate with the core of what it means to live a balanced and meaningful life:

- **Simplicity and Presence:** Learn to let go of clutter—both physical and mental—and embrace the beauty of the present moment.

- **Resilience and Balance:** Discover tools for navigating life's challenges with grace and equanimity, finding stability amidst the chaos.

- **Creativity and Flow:** Unlock your creative potential by tapping into the flow state and approaching your passions with mindfulness.

- **Harmony in Relationships:** Foster deeper connections by practicing compassion, active listening, and mindful communication.

- **Sustaining Zen in a Busy World:** Integrate Zen into your daily routines, adapting its principles to the unique demands of your life.

Each chapter builds on the last, creating a cohesive narrative that guides you from understanding Zen's foundational principles to living them in a way that transforms both your inner and outer worlds.

An Invitation to Begin Again

Zen is not about perfection or achievement; it is about practice. It is about showing up, moment after moment, with a willingness to learn, grow, and begin again. This book is not a destination but a starting point—a place to reflect, experiment, and discover what Zen means to you.

As you embark on this journey, I invite you to approach it with curiosity and openness. You do not need to have all the answers or to "get it right." The beauty of Zen lies in its flexibility and adaptability—it meets you where you are and grows with you over time.

Let this book be a companion, a source of inspiration and guidance as you explore the path of Zen. Whether you are seeking peace, clarity, creativity, or connection, know that the tools and insights you need are already within you. Zen simply helps you uncover them.

A Final Word

In a world that often feels overwhelming, Zen offers a simple yet profound reminder: the present moment is enough. It is in this moment—not in the past or the future—that we find peace, joy, and purpose. By living with mindfulness, balance, and compassion, we create a life that reflects the essence of Zen—a life that is not only well-lived but deeply felt.

As you turn the page and step into the chapters ahead, may you find inspiration, insight, and encouragement to live your own Zen-inspired life. The journey is yours to take, and it begins now.

CHAPTER 1: THE ESSENCE OF ZEN – UNDERSTANDING SIMPLICITY AND HARMONY

The Roots of Zen

Zen's history is as profound as its teachings—
steeped in ancient traditions yet resonating
timelessly with modern life. Its journey across
cultures and centuries reveals a philosophy that
emphasizes simplicity, mindfulness, and a deep
connection to the present moment. To understand Zen is to trace its roots, uncovering the
essence of its transformative power.

The Origins of Zen: From Buddha to Bodhidhar-
ma

Zen finds its origins in the teachings of Sid-
dhartha Gautama, the Buddha, in ancient India.
The Buddha's insights into the causes of suffering and the path to enlightenment formed the
foundation of a spiritual practice that sought
liberation from life's struggles. However, Zen
as a distinct tradition began to take shape centuries later when Buddhism traveled to China,
merging with Taoist philosophy to create Chán
Buddhism. This unique synthesis focused on
direct experience rather than scriptural study,
emphasizing meditation as a means of accessing

profound truths.

The figure of Bodhidharma looms large in Zen's history. Often depicted as a fierce and enigmatic monk, Bodhidharma is credited with introducing Chán Buddhism to China in the 6th century. His teachings stressed self-reliance and disciplined meditation, challenging students to seek enlightenment not through external sources but within themselves. His legendary nine years of meditation facing a wall symbolize the unwavering commitment required to understand the essence of Zen.

The Evolution of Zen: A Journey Across Cultures

As Chán Buddhism flourished in China, it adapted to the cultural and philosophical landscape, integrating elements of Taoism's harmony with nature. This fusion created a practice that celebrated simplicity and directness, rejecting elaborate rituals in favor of accessible, experiential wisdom.

When Chán Buddhism made its way to Japan, it evolved into what we now know as Zen. The

Japanese interpretation refined the philosophy further, emphasizing aesthetics and daily practices as expressions of Zen principles. From the serene beauty of rock gardens to the precise movements of a tea ceremony, these art forms became physical manifestations of Zen's focus on mindfulness and harmony.

The Core Philosophy of Zen

At its heart, Zen is a practice of being present. It teaches that enlightenment is not a distant goal but an experience accessible in the here and now. By stripping away distractions and mental clutter, Zen encourages individuals to see the world as it truly is, unfiltered by judgment or expectation.

Central to Zen's philosophy is the idea of impermanence—a recognition that all things are transient. This understanding fosters a sense of detachment, not in the sense of indifference but as a way to engage with life fully without clinging to outcomes. Zen invites us to embrace change as a natural part of existence, finding peace in the ever-shifting flow of life.

Zen's Relevance Today: A Timeless Path to Clarity

The roots of Zen offer more than historical insight; they provide a timeless guide for modern living. In a world overwhelmed by noise and complexity, Zen's call to simplicity is more relevant than ever. Its principles encourage us to slow down, breathe deeply, and reconnect with what truly matters.

By understanding Zen's origins, we uncover not only its history but also its enduring wisdom—a path to clarity and balance that transcends time and culture. The story of Zen is a reminder that profound truths often lie in the simplest of practices, waiting to be rediscovered in the present moment.

The Core Principles of Zen

At the heart of Zen lies a set of profound yet simple principles, distilled from centuries of practice and reflection. These core ideas—mindfulness, detachment, and harmony with nature—

offer a framework for living a life of clarity and balance. While they may appear deceptively straightforward, their true depth unfolds only through sustained practice and contemplation.

Mindfulness: The Art of Being Present

Mindfulness, often described as the cornerstone of Zen, is the practice of being fully present in each moment. It calls for a focused awareness that transcends the chatter of the mind, allowing individuals to engage with life as it unfolds. In Zen, mindfulness is not confined to meditation; it permeates every aspect of daily life. Whether walking, eating, or working, each action becomes an opportunity to cultivate presence.

This principle finds its roots in the Buddha's teachings, particularly the concept of *sati*, or mindful awareness. By observing one's thoughts, emotions, and sensations without judgment, mindfulness fosters a deeper understanding of oneself and the world. The Japanese Zen master Thích Nhất Hạnh beautifully encapsulated this idea when he wrote, "The present moment is the only time over which we have dominion." For Zen practitioners, this dominion is not about control but about embracing the moment with open-hearted curiosity and acceptance.

In a modern context, mindfulness offers a powerful antidote to the distractions and demands of contemporary life. By anchoring attention in the present, individuals can reduce stress, improve focus, and build a deeper connection to their experiences. For instance, practicing mindful breathing during a stressful meeting or pausing to fully savor a meal can transform mundane moments into profound acts of self-awareness.

Detachment: Freedom Through Non-Attachment

Detachment, another central principle of Zen, is often misunderstood as a cold or indifferent attitude. In reality, Zen detachment is an act of liberation—freeing oneself from clinging to possessions, outcomes, or even identities. It is not about rejecting life but about engaging with it without the weight of expectation or fear of loss.

Zen's emphasis on impermanence underpins this principle. Everything, from the fleeting beauty of a cherry blossom to the ebb and flow of relationships, is subject to change. Embracing this truth allows practitioners to release their grip on what cannot be controlled, finding peace in the flow of life. As the Zen monk Shunryu Suzuki once said, "In the beginner's mind, there are many possibilities; in the expert's mind, there are few." Detachment cultivates this beginner's mind, an openness that allows for growth and discovery.

Practicing detachment does not mean abandoning ambition or love; rather, it involves pursuing goals and nurturing relationships with a sense of freedom. For example, an artist might create without being consumed by the need for acclaim, focusing instead on the joy of the creative process. Similarly, a professional might strive for success while remaining adaptable to change, unburdened by the fear of failure.

Harmony with Nature: Aligning with the World

Zen philosophy is deeply rooted in the natural world, viewing it as both a teacher and a mirror. Nature's rhythms—the ebb and flow of tides, the cycles of growth and decay—reflect the principles of Zen, particularly its embrace of impermanence and interconnectedness. By attuning oneself to these rhythms, Zen encourages a harmonious way of living that respects the balance of all things.

The Zen practice of walking meditation, for example, is a powerful way to connect with nature. In this practice, each step is taken with intention, synchronized with the breath, and aligned with the surroundings. This simple act transforms walking into a sacred ritual, fostering a sense of unity with the environment.

In modern life, where concrete jungles often replace natural landscapes, finding harmony with nature can feel elusive. Yet, even small acts—like tending a plant, gazing at the sky, or listening to the sound of rain—can ground individuals in the present and rekindle their connection to the world around them. Zen reminds us that nature is not separate from us; it is a reflection of our own inner states.

Living the Core Principles

While mindfulness, detachment, and harmony with nature are distinct principles, they are deeply interwoven. Practicing one often leads to the cultivation of the others. For example, mindfulness naturally fosters detachment by revealing the transient nature of thoughts and emotions. Similarly, spending time in nature can enhance mindfulness, creating a feedback loop that reinforces Zen's holistic approach to life.

These principles are not merely philosophical ideals but practical tools for navigating life's complexities. They offer a lens through which to view challenges as opportunities for growth, relationships as mirrors for self-discovery, and everyday routines as acts of mindfulness. By integrating these ideas into daily life, individuals can create a sense of balance that sustains them through change and uncertainty.

The core principles of Zen serve as guideposts on the path to simplicity and harmony. They invite us to slow down, let go, and reconnect with the present moment—a moment that holds infinite potential for peace, clarity, and joy.

Zen in Action – Living Simply

Simplicity, as envisioned by Zen, is not a matter of deprivation or austerity but a conscious choice to focus on what truly matters. It is a way of living that clears the clutter—both physical and mental—allowing clarity, peace, and purpose to take root. Zen transforms simplicity from a passive state of "less" to an active practice of intentionality, where every action is imbued with meaning and mindfulness.

The Zen Aesthetic: Beauty in Simplicity

Zen has long celebrated simplicity as an art form, evident in practices like the Japanese tea ceremony and the creation of rock gardens. These art forms are not about achieving perfection but about embracing imperfection and finding beauty in restraint. In a Zen rock garden, for example, the carefully raked gravel and sparsely placed stones evoke a sense of harmony and balance. The emptiness within the garden is as significant as the elements themselves, illustrating the Zen principle that simplicity creates space for deeper meaning.

This aesthetic of simplicity is more than visual; it is a mindset. It teaches that by paring down the nonessential, we can uncover the profound. Zen invites us to view simplicity as a lens through which to see the world clearly, free from the distractions of excess and superficiality. This perspective can inspire us to approach our lives with the same intentionality, whether designing a home, organizing a workspace, or curating the relationships we nurture.

Decluttering the Physical Space: The Zen of Letting Go

The physical environment profoundly impacts the mind. A cluttered space often mirrors a cluttered mind, making it difficult to focus, relax, or find inspiration. Zen encourages us to create spaces that reflect simplicity and order, fostering a sense of calm and clarity.

The act of decluttering is a Zen practice in itself. It requires mindfulness and a willingness to let go of what no longer serves us. For instance, when approaching a cluttered room, the Zen practitioner might ask, "Does this object bring joy or utility to my life?" If the answer is no, the object is released with gratitude, making room for what truly matters.

Decluttering is not about achieving a sterile environment but about cultivating a space that supports mindfulness and intentional living. A clean, open space becomes a canvas for creativity and relaxation, free from the distractions of unnecessary possessions. This practice extends beyond the home to workplaces and even digital environments, where decluttering can create a sense of focus and efficiency.

Clearing the Mental Space: A Quiet Mind

While physical clutter is often the first to be addressed, Zen recognizes that mental clutter can be even more insidious. The constant chatter of the mind—worries, judgments, and distractions—obscures our ability to live fully in the present. Zen teaches that by simplifying our mental landscape, we can achieve a state of clarity and inner peace.

Meditation is one of Zen's primary tools for

clearing the mind. By sitting in stillness and focusing on the breath, practitioners learn to observe their thoughts without attachment, allowing them to pass like clouds in the sky. This practice, known as *zazen*, helps to cultivate a quiet mind and a heightened awareness of the present moment.

Another technique is the practice of mindfulness, where everyday actions become opportunities for mental clarity. For example, washing dishes is no longer a mundane chore but an act of presence: feeling the water, observing the soap bubbles, and immersing oneself fully in the task. This simple shift in perspective transforms routine activities into moments of Zen, reducing mental clutter and fostering a sense of peace.

The Joy of Living Simply

Zen's approach to simplicity is not about sacrifice but about liberation. By letting go of what is unnecessary, we create space for what truly matters—peace, connection, and purpose. This philosophy resonates deeply in a world where the pursuit of more often leaves us feeling overwhelmed and dissatisfied.

Living simply does not mean rejecting the modern world or its conveniences. Instead, it involves making conscious choices about what we allow into our lives. For some, this might mean owning fewer possessions; for others, it might mean setting boundaries around time and energy. The key is to prioritize what aligns with one's values and aspirations, letting go of distractions that detract from those goals.

Historically, Zen monks exemplified this principle by embracing a life of minimalism. Their robes, bowls, and few possessions were carefully chosen for their utility, reflecting a commitment to simplicity and mindfulness. This lifestyle was not about self-denial but about creating the freedom to focus on spiritual practice and personal growth.

For modern readers, the joy of living simply can be found in small, intentional steps. Decluttering a closet, reducing commitments, or practicing gratitude for the essentials are all ways to embrace Zen simplicity. These actions, though modest, ripple outward, creating a sense of balance and fulfillment that permeates every aspect of life.

Conclusion: Simplicity as a Practice

Zen in action is not an abstract ideal but a practical way of living. It teaches that simplicity is not achieved overnight but cultivated through consistent practice. Each act of letting go, each moment of mindfulness, and each effort to declutter—whether physical or mental—brings us closer to a life of clarity and harmony.

As we simplify, we uncover the essence of what truly matters. We find that life's greatest joys often lie in the quiet moments, the simple pleasures, and the connections that arise when we make space for them. Living simply is not an end but a journey, one that aligns us with the core principles of Zen and invites us to experience the richness of life in its most unadorned and authentic form.

Harmony with the World

Zen teaches that the world is not something separate from us; we are intrinsically part of its rhythms and cycles. Achieving harmony with the world begins with recognizing this interconnectedness and aligning our actions with the natural order. In a chaotic and often disorienting environment, this principle offers a path to balance and serenity.

The Natural Order: Lessons from Nature

In Zen, nature is not merely a backdrop but a profound teacher. The cycles of the seasons, the flow of rivers, and the rise and fall of mountains embody the principles of impermanence, balance, and resilience. By observing these patterns, we learn to live in greater harmony with ourselves and the world.

One Zen proverb states, "Sitting quietly, doing nothing, spring comes, and the grass grows by itself." This simple yet profound observation underscores the idea that life unfolds naturally when we align with its rhythms rather than resist them. Just as the grass grows without effort, we, too, can find ease by living in accordance with the world's natural flow.

For example, consider the tides of the ocean,

which ebb and flow in response to the gravitational pull of the moon. This dance of water and celestial body is a reminder that harmony arises not from control but from attunement. When we embrace this perspective, we can approach life's challenges with a sense of fluidity and adaptability, navigating change as naturally as water finds its course.

Finding Balance in a Chaotic World

The modern world often feels disconnected from the natural rhythms that Zen cherishes. The constant hum of technology, the pace of urban life, and the pressures of work create an environment that feels anything but harmonious. Yet, even in this chaos, Zen offers tools to cultivate balance.

One way to find harmony is to simplify our interactions with the world. This does not mean retreating from society but approaching it with mindfulness and intention. For instance, practicing gratitude for small, daily experiences—a kind word, the warmth of the sun, or the scent of fresh air—grounds us in the present and reminds us of our connection to the world around us.

Another strategy is to create rituals that restore balance. This might involve spending time in nature, whether walking in a park or sitting beneath a tree, allowing the natural world to recalibrate our senses. Even a few moments of stillness each day can help us reconnect with the world's harmony, creating a sense of inner calm that persists amidst external chaos.

Acting in Alignment with the World

Harmony with the world is not just about observing nature's principles but living in accordance with them. Zen teaches that our actions should reflect the interconnectedness of all things, fostering a sense of responsibility and care for the world we inhabit.

This philosophy is evident in the concept of *samu*, or mindful work, which Zen monks practice as part of their daily routine. Whether sweeping the temple grounds or preparing meals, each task is approached with full attention and a sense of service. This practice reinforces the idea that every action, no matter how small, contributes to the greater whole.

In modern life, acting in alignment with the world might involve making choices that prioritize sustainability and kindness. For example, consuming less, supporting ethical practices, and treating others with compassion are ways to live in harmony with the environment and the broader community. These actions, while seemingly modest, create ripples that extend far beyond the individual, fostering a world that is more balanced and connected.

The Interplay of Inner and Outer Harmony

Zen emphasizes that inner harmony and harmony with the world are deeply intertwined. When we cultivate peace within ourselves, we naturally bring that peace into our interactions with others and the environment. Conversely, aligning with the world's rhythms can help us find balance internally.

For instance, the practice of mindful breathing connects the inner and outer worlds. Each breath is a reminder of our dependence on the air, the trees, and the ecosystems that sustain life. This simple act of awareness bridges the gap between the individual and the collective, reinforcing the Zen principle of interconnectedness.

In relationships, harmony with the world translates into mindful communication and empathy. By truly listening to others and responding with compassion, we create connections that reflect Zen's values of unity and balance. This approach not only nurtures healthier relationships but also contributes to a more harmonious world.

The Transformative Power of Harmony

Living in harmony with the world transforms more than just the individual—it has the potential to create a ripple effect that inspires change. When we align our actions with the natural order, we set an example for others, demonstrating that peace and balance are not only possible but profoundly impactful.

Consider the story of Zen master Ryokan, who lived a life of simplicity and harmony. Legend has it that one night, a thief broke into his hut, only to find there was nothing to steal. Ryokan, noticing the thief's plight, offered him the clothes off his back, saying, "If only I could give you this beautiful moon." This act of kindness and detachment exemplifies the Zen ideal of living in harmony with the world, responding to life's challenges with grace and compassion.

For modern readers, the lesson is clear: harmony begins with small, intentional actions that reflect an awareness of our place in the world. By living simply, acting mindfully, and fostering connections, we contribute to a world that is more aligned with Zen's principles of balance and unity.

Conclusion: A Path to Balance and Serenity

Harmony with the world is not a destination but a journey—a continuous practice of aligning with nature's rhythms and embracing life's interconnectedness. In a chaotic and fragmented world, Zen offers a timeless path to balance and serenity, reminding us that we are not separate from the world but an integral part of its unfolding.

As we integrate this principle into our lives, we

find that harmony is not something we achieve but something we live. It is the quiet joy of being in tune with the world, the peace that comes from simplicity, and the fulfillment of knowing that our actions reflect the beauty and balance of life itself.

CHAPTER 2: THE POWER OF PRESENCE – FINDING CALM IN THE CHAOS

What It Means to Be Present

The present moment is the only place where life truly unfolds. It is where the fullness of existence resides—unfiltered by the regrets of the past or the anxieties of the future. Yet, in a world dominated by constant distractions, the simple act of being present has become a profound challenge. Zen teaches that cultivating mindfulness—the art of fully inhabiting the here and now—is not only the foundation of inner peace but also a gateway to understanding life's deeper truths.

The Nature of Presence

To be present is to experience life as it is, free from the filters of judgment, expectation, or distraction. This state of awareness allows us to engage with each moment fully, whether it is a moment of joy, sorrow, or quiet reflection. In Zen, presence is not something to achieve but to realize—it is a state that already exists within us, waiting to be uncovered.

The 13th-century Zen master Dōgen described this idea in his teachings on *shikantaza*, or "just sitting." This form of meditation involves sitting without striving, simply observing the flow of thoughts and sensations without attachment. Dōgen's teachings emphasize that presence is not about controlling the mind but about letting go of the need to control, allowing awareness to emerge naturally.

Presence is also deeply embodied. It is not confined to the mind but encompasses the entire sensory experience. The sound of the wind in the trees, the warmth of the sun on the skin, and the rhythm of one's own breath are all aspects of the present moment. Zen reminds us that by grounding ourselves in these sensations, we can find a direct connection to life's essence.

The Obstacles to Presence

Despite its simplicity, being present often feels elusive. The mind, conditioned to wander, pulls us toward memories of the past or anticipations of the future. This constant mental chatter creates a barrier between ourselves and the reality of the moment. In Zen, this phenomenon is referred to as the "monkey mind," a restless and unfocused state that keeps us from fully engaging with life.

Modern life amplifies these challenges. The rapid pace of work, the endless scroll of social media, and the omnipresence of digital notifications create an environment where attention is perpetually fragmented. These distractions not only hinder our ability to be present but also leave us feeling overwhelmed and disconnected.

Yet, Zen teaches that these obstacles are not insurmountable. By cultivating mindfulness, we can learn to quiet the monkey mind and reclaim our connection to the present. This process begins with a simple yet profound shift in perspective: recognizing that the present moment is not something to escape but something to embrace.

Cultivating Mindfulness

Mindfulness is the practice of bringing one's full attention to the present moment, observing thoughts, feelings, and sensations without judgment. It is not about emptying the mind or forcing a state of calm but about cultivating a gentle awareness that allows us to see things as they are.

One way to develop mindfulness is through the practice of focused breathing. By directing attention to the rhythm of the breath—the rise and fall of the chest, the sensation of air entering and leaving the nostrils—we create an anchor that grounds us in the here and now. This practice, though simple, has a profound effect on the mind, reducing stress and enhancing clarity.

Another method is to approach everyday activities with mindfulness. Tasks that might otherwise be performed on autopilot, such as washing dishes or walking, become opportunities for presence when done with intention. For instance, washing dishes can transform from a mundane chore into a meditative act: feeling the warmth of the water, noticing the texture of the soap bubbles, and immersing oneself fully in the experience.

Mindfulness also involves observing thoughts and emotions without becoming entangled in them. This practice, known in Zen as *kanshiketsu* or "viewing the mind," helps us recognize the transient nature of mental states. By seeing thoughts as passing clouds rather than fixed realities, we cultivate a sense of detachment that allows us to respond to life with greater equanimity.

The Transformative Power of Presence

The practice of mindfulness is not just a means to an end; it is transformative in itself. By anchoring ourselves in the present, we discover a richness and depth that often goes unnoticed. The ordinary becomes extraordinary: a sunrise is no longer a background event but a moment of profound beauty, and a conversation becomes an opportunity for genuine connection.

Presence also fosters resilience. When we are fully present, we face life's challenges with clarity and courage, unburdened by the weight of past regrets or future fears. This mindset allows us to navigate difficulties with grace, finding solutions and insights that emerge only in the stillness of the moment.

For many, the practice of mindfulness leads to a deeper sense of gratitude. By focusing on what is rather than what was or what could be, we cultivate an appreciation for life's simple pleasures. The laughter of a friend, the aroma of freshly brewed tea, or the feel of grass underfoot become sources of joy and contentment.

Conclusion: Presence as a Way of Being

To be present is to live fully. It is a practice that reconnects us with the essence of who we are and the world around us. In a society that often pulls us in countless directions, mindfulness offers a path back to ourselves, a way to find calm in the chaos.

As we continue exploring the power of presence in this chapter, we will uncover practical tools and strategies for grounding ourselves, over-coming distractions, and reaping the rewards of mindful living. But at its core, the journey begins with a simple realization: the present moment is all we ever truly have. By embracing it, we unlock the boundless potential of life itself.

Practices for Grounding Yourself

In the swirling chaos of modern life, grounding oneself is an act of reclamation—a way of finding stability amid the turbulence. Zen offers a wealth of practices to anchor us in the present moment, helping us reconnect with the here and now. These techniques are not abstract exercises but practical tools that anyone can use to cultivate a sense of calm and presence, no matter the circumstances.

Meditation: The Foundation of Grounding

At the heart of Zen lies meditation, a practice that invites stillness and introspection. Known as *zazen*, or seated meditation, this cornerstone of Zen practice provides a sanctuary for the mind and body. Unlike practices aimed at achieving a specific state, *zazen* encourages practitioners to simply sit and observe, allowing thoughts to come and go without attachment.

Zen master Dōgen described meditation as "thinking of not-thinking." This paradoxical phrase captures the essence of grounding: letting go of the effort to control the mind and instead resting in awareness. By focusing on the breath, practitioners create an anchor that steadies the mind. Each inhale and exhale becomes a reminder of the body's connection to the present moment, a lifeline amidst the currents of thought and emotion.

In a modern context, even a few minutes of meditation can offer profound benefits. Sitting quietly, closing the eyes, and focusing on the natural rhythm of the breath can create a sense of grounding that carries into the rest of the day. Over time, this practice cultivates a calm and centered presence, transforming the way one approaches life's challenges.

Breathwork: Harnessing the Power of the Breath

Breathwork is another powerful tool for grounding, rooted in the understanding that the breath is both a physical and spiritual bridge between the inner and outer worlds. Zen teaches that conscious breathing connects us to the present moment, calming the mind and energizing the body.

A simple yet effective technique is *hara breathing*, which focuses on the lower abdomen, or *hara*, considered the body's center of gravity in Zen. To practice, one places a hand on the lower abdomen and takes slow, deep breaths, feeling the rise and fall of this area. This method not only steadies the mind but also promotes a sense of stability and balance.

Another approach, borrowed from the Zen-inspired mindfulness movement, is the 4-7-8 breathing technique. Inhaling deeply for a count of four, holding the breath for seven, and exhaling slowly for eight creates a calming rhythm that soothes the nervous system. This practice can be particularly helpful during moments of stress, offering an immediate way to ground oneself.

Body Scanning: Anchoring Awareness in the Body

Zen recognizes the body as a vessel for awareness, emphasizing the importance of grounding through physical sensation. Body scanning, a meditative technique, involves directing attention to different parts of the body, observing sensations without judgment. This practice fosters a sense of connection and presence, helping individuals move out of their heads and into their bodies.

To perform a body scan, one begins by sitting or
lying down in a comfortable position. Closing
the eyes, attention is brought to the toes, noticing any tension, warmth, or other sensations.
Gradually, awareness moves upward through
the legs, torso, arms, and head, pausing at each
area to observe without trying to change anything. This gentle exploration of the body creates a profound sense of grounding, offering
relief from the fragmented awareness that often
accompanies stress.

In addition to promoting mindfulness, body
scanning can reveal areas of tension or discomfort, encouraging a deeper connection to
physical well-being. Regular practice can help
individuals become more attuned to their bodies, fostering a sense of wholeness and presence.

**The Role of Movement: Grounding Through
Action**

While stillness is a key aspect of grounding,
movement also plays an essential role. Practices
such as walking meditation combine the bene-

fits of mindfulness with the grounding effects of physical activity. In walking meditation, each step is taken with intention, synchronized with the breath. The sensation of the feet meeting the ground becomes a focal point, creating a rhythm that grounds the mind in the body.

This practice is particularly effective for those who find sitting meditation challenging. It offers a dynamic way to cultivate presence, turning even a short walk into an opportunity for grounding. Whether practiced in a quiet garden or along a bustling sidewalk, walking meditation transforms movement into a meditative act.

For those drawn to more vigorous forms of movement, practices like yoga or tai chi also align with Zen principles. These disciplines emphasize the connection between breath and motion, fostering a sense of flow and grounding that extends beyond the practice itself.

Practical Applications for Everyday Life

Grounding practices are not confined to formal meditation or structured exercises; they can be seamlessly integrated into daily life. For example, pausing to take a few deep breaths before a meeting or during a stressful commute can create a moment of stillness in the midst of activity. Similarly, paying attention to the sensation of water on the skin while washing hands or the sound of footsteps while walking transforms ordinary tasks into grounding rituals.

Another simple yet profound practice is to connect with nature. Standing barefoot on the earth, feeling the texture of grass or sand beneath the feet, is a direct way to ground oneself physically and energetically. Even small interactions with nature, such as tending a plant or gazing at the sky, can foster a sense of connection and presence.

Conclusion: Grounding as a Way of Being

Grounding is more than a collection of techniques; it is a way of being that aligns the mind, body, and spirit with the present moment. By cultivating practices like meditation, breathwork, body scanning, and mindful movement, we create a foundation of stability and calm that supports us through life's inevitable chaos.

These practices are not about escaping the world but about engaging with it fully and authentically. They remind us that grounding is not a destination but a practice—a continual return to the here and now. As we explore these techniques and make them a part of our daily lives, we discover the transformative power of presence, finding calm and clarity in the midst of life's ever-changing currents.

Overcoming Modern Distractions

In a world saturated with notifications, advertisements, and endless streams of information, distractions have become a defining challenge of modern life. They pull us away from the present moment, fragmenting our attention and leaving us feeling scattered and overwhelmed. Zen offers timeless insights and practical strategies to navigate this landscape, reclaiming our focus and cultivating a sense of calm amidst the noise.

The Nature of Distraction

Distraction is not a modern phenomenon—it is a universal aspect of the human experience. Even in ancient times, Zen practitioners recognized the mind's tendency to wander, likening it to a monkey leaping from branch to branch. What sets today's distractions apart, however, is their sheer volume and intensity. The proliferation of digital technology has created a world where attention is constantly under siege, with algorithms designed to capture and hold our focus at any cost.

This endless barrage of stimuli can have profound effects on the mind. Studies have shown that multitasking, for instance, diminishes cognitive performance, while constant notifications increase stress levels. Beyond the immediate impacts, living in a state of perpetual distraction erodes our ability to be present, depriving us of the depth and richness that comes from fully engaging with life.

Zen teaches that the first step to overcoming

distraction is awareness—recognizing the forces that pull us away from the present and understanding their impact. By cultivating this awareness, we can begin to make conscious choices about where and how we direct our attention.

The Power of Single-Tasking

One of Zen's most powerful antidotes to distraction is single-tasking: the practice of focusing on one activity at a time. This approach is rooted in the principle of mindfulness, which encourages us to bring our full attention to the task at hand. Whether it is brewing a cup of tea, writing an email, or listening to a friend, single-tasking transforms ordinary actions into acts of presence.

Consider the Zen tradition of the tea ceremony, where every step—from heating the water to whisking the matcha—is performed with meticulous attention. This ritual, though simple, exemplifies the power of single-tasking to create a sense of clarity and connection. By fully immersing ourselves in each moment, we not only improve the quality of our work but also deepen our appreciation for the experience itself.

In daily life, embracing single-tasking might mean turning off notifications while working, setting aside dedicated time for specific activities, or practicing mindful eating without the distraction of screens. These small changes can have a profound impact, allowing us to reclaim our focus and engage more fully with our surroundings.

Managing Technology Mindfully

Technology is both a source of distraction and a tool for mindfulness—it all depends on how we use it. Zen invites us to approach technology with intention, leveraging its benefits while minimizing its potential to overwhelm. This begins with creating boundaries around digital consumption.

For example, establishing "tech-free zones" in the home—such as the dining table or bedroom—can help create spaces for uninterrupted presence. Similarly, setting specific times for checking email or social media reduces the impulse to constantly reach for devices, freeing up mental bandwidth for more meaningful pursuits.

Another powerful practice is to periodically disconnect entirely, embracing moments of digital silence. Whether it is a few hours or an entire day, stepping away from screens allows us to reset and reconnect with the physical world. These breaks are not about rejecting technology but about restoring balance, ensuring that it serves us rather than dominates us.

Zen also encourages mindful engagement with technology. This might involve pausing before opening an app to consider whether it aligns with our intentions or using tools like mindfulness apps to support meditative practices. By approaching technology with awareness, we transform it from a source of distraction into an ally on the path to presence.

Navigating Multitasking and Overcommitment

In a culture that often equates busyness with productivity, multitasking has become a badge of honor. Yet, research consistently shows that dividing attention between multiple tasks reduces efficiency and increases errors. Zen challenges this paradigm, advocating for a slower, more deliberate approach to work and life.

The practice of *shoshin*, or beginner's mind, offers a valuable perspective. In Zen, beginner's mind refers to approaching each task with curiosity and openness, as if encountering it for the first time. This mindset encourages us to fully engage with one activity at a time, free from the urge to rush or juggle competing priorities.

In practical terms, this might involve setting realistic goals for the day, prioritizing tasks, and saying no to commitments that do not align with our values. It also means recognizing the limits of our attention and giving ourselves permission to rest when needed. By embracing this slower, more intentional pace, we not only improve our focus but also enhance our overall well-being.

Reconnecting with the Present Moment

At its core, overcoming distraction is about returning to the present moment. Zen teaches that the present is not something we need to seek; it is always available, waiting for us to notice. The challenge lies in choosing to turn our attention toward it.

One way to reconnect is through the practice of pausing. Throughout the day, taking brief moments to pause and observe the breath, body, or surroundings creates a thread of mindfulness that weaves through even the busiest schedules. These pauses, though fleeting, serve as anchors, reminding us of our capacity for presence.

Another approach is to cultivate gratitude for the present moment. By acknowledging the beauty and abundance of what is already here—a kind word, a ray of sunlight, or the taste of fresh fruit—we shift our focus from what distracts us to what nourishes us. This practice not only reduces the allure of distractions but also deepens our appreciation for life's simple joys.

Conclusion: A Path to Clarity and Focus

Distractions are an inevitable part of life, but they need not define our experience. By cultivating awareness, embracing single-tasking, and

approaching technology with intention, we create space for presence in even the most chaotic
environments. These practices, though rooted in
Zen's ancient wisdom, are profoundly relevant
in today's world, offering a path to clarity and
focus amidst the noise.

As we integrate these strategies into our daily
lives, we discover that the power of presence
is not about escaping distraction but about reclaiming our attention. It is about choosing to be
fully here, fully alive, in each moment—transforming the chaos of modern life into an opportunity for mindfulness, connection, and growth.

Reaping the Rewards of Presence

The rewards of presence are as profound as
they are transformative. To live mindfully is to
uncover a depth of experience that often goes
unnoticed, to access a reservoir of clarity, peace,
and resilience. These benefits extend beyond
the individual, influencing relationships, decision-making, and overall well-being. In the
practice of presence, we find not just a method
for coping with chaos but a way of thriving

within it.

The Mental Clarity of Mindfulness

One of the most immediate rewards of presence is mental clarity. By focusing on the here and now, we quiet the mental chatter that clouds judgment and perspective. This clarity allows us to see situations as they truly are, uncolored by past regrets or future anxieties. It creates space for thoughtful responses rather than reactive impulses, a hallmark of inner fortitude.

Consider the experience of a Zen monk tending to a garden. Each action—pruning a branch, raking gravel, or watering a plant—is performed with full attention. This deliberate focus mirrors the mental clarity that arises from mindfulness, a state where distractions fall away, and the mind becomes as calm and ordered as the garden itself.

For modern practitioners, this clarity manifests in various ways: the ability to approach challenges with a calm and steady mind, to prioritize tasks effectively, and to make decisions with confidence. Mindfulness does not eliminate life's complexities, but it equips us with the tools to navigate them with grace.

Emotional Resilience Through Presence

Living mindfully also cultivates emotional resilience, the capacity to endure and adapt to life's ups and downs. In Zen, this resilience is rooted in the practice of observing emotions without becoming entangled in them. By acknowledging feelings as they arise—whether joy, sadness, anger, or fear—we create a sense of detachment that prevents us from being swept away.

This principle is beautifully illustrated in the Zen teaching of "sitting with what is." Rather than resisting or suppressing difficult emotions, practitioners are encouraged to sit with them, much like sitting quietly with a storm. The storm will pass, and in its wake, a sense of calm and clarity will emerge.

For contemporary readers, this practice translates into a healthier relationship with emotions. Instead of avoiding discomfort or seeking constant distraction, mindfulness invites us to face emotions directly, building the strength to weather life's challenges. Over time, this approach fosters a sense of inner stability, a confidence that we can handle whatever comes our way.

Physical Benefits of Mindful Living

The connection between mind and body is a central tenet of Zen, and the physical benefits of mindfulness are well-documented. Studies have shown that practices like meditation and deep breathing reduce stress, lower blood pressure, and improve sleep quality. These effects are not incidental but a reflection of the body's natural response to presence.

When we live mindfully, we become attuned to the body's needs, recognizing signals of tension, fatigue, or imbalance. This awareness encourages healthier choices, from eating more consciously to resting when needed. It also enhances the body's ability to heal and regenerate, a testament to the profound interplay between mindfulness and physical well-being.

The physical rewards of presence extend beyond health to include a sense of vitality and connection. By grounding ourselves in the sensations of the present—feeling the warmth of the sun, the rhythm of the breath, or the solidity of the earth beneath our feet—we reconnect with the body as a source of strength and aliveness.

Strengthening Relationships Through Mindful Connection

The practice of presence transforms not only the self but also the way we relate to others. Mindfulness enhances empathy, compassion, and the ability to listen deeply, creating relationships that are more meaningful and authentic.

In Zen, the act of listening is often described as "listening with the whole being." This means being fully present with another person, free from distractions or preconceived judgments. Whether in a conversation with a friend, a colleague, or a loved one, this level of attention fosters trust and understanding, strengthening the bonds that connect us.

For example, consider the impact of mindful communication in resolving conflict. By approaching disagreements with curiosity and openness rather than defensiveness, we create space for mutual understanding and resolution. This approach not only diffuses tension but also deepens the relationship, turning moments of discord into opportunities for growth.

A Sense of Purpose and Fulfillment

At its core, mindfulness reconnects us with a sense of purpose and fulfillment. By focusing on the present, we uncover the richness of life's simplest moments—a child's laughter, the taste of a favorite meal, or the beauty of a sunset. These moments, often overlooked in the rush of daily life, become sources of profound joy and gratitude.

Zen teaches that fulfillment is not found in the pursuit of external achievements but in the act of fully living each moment. This perspective challenges the notion that happiness lies somewhere in the future, reminding us that the present is not a means to an end but an end in itself.

For many, this shift in perspective brings a sense of liberation. By releasing the constant striving for "more," we discover that what we have—

and who we are—is enough. This realization fosters contentment and peace, a reward that transcends the material and reaches the spiritual.

Conclusion: A Life Enriched by Presence

The rewards of presence are far-reaching, touching every aspect of life. From mental clarity and emotional resilience to physical vitality and deeper connections, mindfulness offers a path to living fully and authentically. These benefits are not fleeting but enduring, growing stronger with each moment of practice.

As we reap the rewards of presence, we also contribute to the world around us. A calm and centered mind inspires others, a compassionate heart nurtures relationships, and a mindful approach to life creates ripples of positivity that extend far beyond the self.

In the practice of presence, we find not only a way to navigate chaos but a way to transform it. The journey is not about perfection but about progress—a continual return to the here and now, where life unfolds in all its depth and beauty. Through mindfulness, we unlock the power of presence, discovering that the greatest rewards are not what we achieve but how we experience the world, moment by moment.

CHAPTER 3: BALANCE THROUGH DISCIPLINE – CULTIVATING DAILY ZEN PRACTICES

The Role of Discipline in Zen

Discipline is often misunderstood as a rigid adherence to rules or an unyielding display of self-control. In Zen, however, discipline is seen as a path to freedom—a way to cultivate balance, clarity, and purpose. Far from being restrictive, it is the foundation upon which the practice of mindfulness and presence is built, enabling individuals to transcend chaos and live with intention.

The Zen Perspective on Discipline

At its core, Zen discipline is not about forcing oneself to conform to external standards but about aligning one's actions with inner values. It is the consistent effort to live in harmony with the principles of simplicity, mindfulness, and compassion. This approach transforms discipline from an act of obligation into an act of devotion—a commitment to the practice of being fully alive.

Zen practitioners often speak of discipline as a form of self-respect. By dedicating time and energy to practices like meditation, mindful work, or silent reflection, they honor their commitment to self-awareness and growth. This perspective reframes discipline as an act of love rather than duty, emphasizing its role in nurturing the mind, body, and spirit.

One of the guiding principles of Zen discipline is the concept of *shugyō*, which translates to "training" or "practice." This term reflects the understanding that discipline is not a destination but a continuous process—a journey of refinement and discovery. Through consistent effort, practitioners cultivate a sense of mastery over themselves and their environment, creating a foundation for deeper insight and peace.

Historical Roots of Zen Discipline

The emphasis on discipline in Zen can be traced back to its origins in Buddhist monastic traditions. Monks and nuns adhered to strict codes of conduct, dedicating their lives to meditation, study, and service. This structured way of living was not seen as restrictive but as a means of creating the conditions necessary for enlightenment.

One of the most striking examples of Zen discipline is the practice of *sesshin*, or intensive meditation retreats. During these retreats, participants engage in long hours of seated meditation, often punctuated by brief periods of walking meditation or mindful work. The schedule is demanding, yet it is designed to strip away distractions and immerse participants fully in the practice of presence. For many, the discipline of *sesshin* becomes a transformative experience, revealing the power of consistent effort to break through mental and emotional barriers.

The story of Zen master Hakuin Ekaku offers a compelling illustration of this principle. Hakuin, one of the most influential figures in Japanese Zen, underwent years of rigorous training to overcome his doubts and achieve clarity. His unwavering dedication to his practice became a hallmark of his teachings, inspiring countless students to embrace discipline as a path to liberation.

The Paradox of Effort and Non-Effort

Zen discipline is often described as a paradox: it requires effort, yet it is not about striving. This concept is encapsulated in the practice of *zazen*, or seated meditation, where practitioners are encouraged to sit with a sense of ease and openness rather than forcing themselves into a particular state of mind.

This balance between effort and non-effort is at the heart of Zen discipline. It teaches that while consistency and commitment are essential, they must be tempered with acceptance and patience. For example, a practitioner may set aside time each day for meditation, but the goal is not to "achieve" anything during that time. Instead, the act of showing up and engaging with the practice becomes the reward itself.

This principle extends beyond meditation to all aspects of life. Whether learning a skill, pursuing a career, or building relationships, the Zen approach to discipline emphasizes steady, intentional effort without attachment to outcomes.

This mindset allows individuals to persevere through challenges with resilience and grace, trusting that the process will yield its own rewards.

Practical Applications of Zen Discipline

For modern readers, the role of discipline in Zen offers valuable insights into how to navigate life's demands with clarity and focus. One of the key takeaways is the importance of creating routines that support mindfulness and balance. These routines need not be elaborate; even small, consistent actions—like setting aside time for quiet reflection or committing to mindful eating—can have a profound impact.

Another practical application is the cultivation of what Zen calls "beginner's mind." This concept, introduced by Zen master Shunryu Suzuki, encourages practitioners to approach each task with curiosity and openness, free from the burden of expectations or preconceptions. By embracing this mindset, individuals can transform even mundane activities into opportunities for growth and presence.

Zen discipline also involves setting boundaries, both external and internal. This might mean limiting distractions, such as turning off notifications during meditation, or recognizing when to say no to commitments that do not align with one's values. By prioritizing what truly matters, discipline becomes a tool for creating a life of purpose and fulfillment.

The Freedom Found in Discipline

The ultimate reward of Zen discipline is freedom—the freedom to live authentically, to engage fully with the present moment, and to respond to life's challenges with equanimity. This freedom arises not from avoiding effort but from embracing it, recognizing that discipline is not a constraint but a pathway to self-mastery.

Zen teaches that true freedom is not the absence of boundaries but the ability to choose one's path with intention and clarity. Through consistent practice, we cultivate the skills and resilience needed to navigate life's complexities, finding balance and harmony in the midst of chaos.

Conclusion: Discipline as a Way of Life

Discipline in Zen is not a rigid framework but a dynamic and compassionate practice that evolves over time. It is a way of aligning with one's values, cultivating presence, and creating the conditions for inner peace and growth. By embracing the role of discipline in our lives, we open ourselves to its transformative power, discovering that consistent effort is not a burden but a gift.

As we continue to explore daily rituals, habit formation, and the balance between structure and flexibility in the following sections, the foundation of discipline will remain central—a guiding light on the path to a life of mindfulness, balance, and fulfillment.

Daily Rituals for a Balanced Life

In Zen, the rhythm of daily life is not a series of tasks to be completed but a sacred dance of mindfulness and intention. Each moment, no matter how mundane, is an opportunity to cultivate balance, clarity, and harmony. Daily rituals—rooted in Zen principles—serve as anchors, guiding us through the ebb and flow of life while fostering a deeper connection to ourselves and the world around us.

The Zen Approach to Rituals

Rituals in Zen are not about rigid adherence to routines but about infusing ordinary actions with mindfulness and purpose. Whether it is preparing a meal, sweeping the floor, or sipping tea, these practices transform the mundane into the meaningful. The intention behind the action is what matters most, turning even the simplest tasks into expressions of balance and presence.

Zen master Thích Nhất Hạnh often described rituals as "bells of mindfulness," moments that call us back to the present. For example, the sound of a bell in a meditation hall signals a pause, inviting practitioners to take a deep breath and reconnect with the here and now. Similarly, daily rituals serve as touchstones, helping us navigate the complexities of modern life with greater ease and awareness.

Mindful Eating: Nourishment Beyond the Plate

One of the most accessible Zen-inspired rituals is mindful eating. In our fast-paced world, meals are often rushed or consumed alongside distractions like scrolling through a phone or watching television. Zen invites us to approach eating as a meditative practice, a way to connect with the present moment and honor the nourishment we receive.

In a traditional Zen monastery, meals are eaten in silence, with each bite savored slowly. This practice cultivates gratitude for the food and the effort that went into its preparation. It also fosters a deeper awareness of the body's needs, encouraging balanced and intentional choices.

To bring mindful eating into daily life, one can begin by pausing before a meal to take a few deep breaths. Observing the colors, textures, and aromas of the food creates a sense of anticipation and appreciation. As you eat, focusing on the taste and sensation of each bite helps to anchor your attention, transforming the act of eating into a ritual of presence and gratitude.

Mindful Movement: The Body in Harmony

Zen emphasizes the importance of connecting with the body, not only through stillness but also through movement. Practices like walking meditation and mindful stretching integrate the principles of balance and discipline into physical activity, creating a sense of harmony between mind and body.

Walking meditation, or *kinhin*, is a cornerstone of Zen practice. During this ritual, practitioners walk slowly and deliberately, syncing each step with their breath. The sensation of the feet touching the ground becomes a focal point, grounding the mind in the body. Whether practiced in a serene garden or along a busy street, walking meditation transforms movement into a form of mindfulness, a way to reconnect with the present.

For those seeking more dynamic forms of movement, yoga and tai chi offer complementary practices. These disciplines emphasize flow and intentionality, encouraging practitioners to move with awareness and grace. Incorporating mindful movement into daily life—whether through a morning stretch, an evening walk, or even a few minutes of standing meditation— enhances physical vitality while grounding the mind.

Creating Rituals for Daily Life

Zen rituals are deeply personal, reflecting the unique rhythms and needs of each individual. The key is to start small, choosing one or two practices that resonate and building from there. Consistency is more important than complexity; even a few minutes of mindful practice each day can have a transformative impact.

For instance, a morning ritual might involve lighting a candle and taking a moment of silence to set an intention for the day. This simple act creates a sense of purpose and focus, a reminder to approach the day with mindfulness and balance. Similarly, an evening ritual might include journaling about the day's experiences or practicing gratitude for moments of joy or learning.

Another powerful ritual is the practice of pausing. Throughout the day, setting aside brief moments to breathe deeply, observe your surroundings, or simply rest in stillness can create a thread of mindfulness that weaves through even the busiest schedules. These pauses are like stepping stones, helping us stay grounded as we navigate the demands of life.

Rituals as Acts of Renewal

In Zen, rituals are not static routines but dynamic practices that evolve over time. They are acts of renewal, opportunities to return to the present and reconnect with what matters most. This perspective transforms rituals from obligations into gifts—moments of self-care and reflection that enrich our lives.

For example, tending to a garden can be a ritual of renewal. Each act, from planting seeds to watering and pruning, becomes a meditation on growth and impermanence. The garden itself becomes a metaphor for life, a reminder that balance and discipline are essential for both flourishing and resilience.

Similarly, cleaning a space can be a ritual of renewal. In Zen, cleaning is not seen as a chore but as a practice of creating harmony. Whether dusting a shelf or organizing a desk, these actions reflect an intention to cultivate order and clarity, both externally and internally.

The Balance of Ritual and Spontaneity

While rituals provide structure, Zen also emphasizes the importance of spontaneity. The goal is not to become rigidly attached to routines but to use them as a foundation for freedom. By cultivating discipline through rituals, we create the stability needed to embrace life's unpredictability with openness and flexibility.

For instance, a morning meditation ritual might be followed by an unstructured walk in nature, allowing for moments of discovery and inspiration. This interplay between ritual and spontaneity mirrors the balance that Zen seeks to cultivate—a harmony between structure and flow.

Conclusion: The Transformative Power of Rituals

Daily rituals are more than habits; they are expressions of mindfulness and intention, pathways to a balanced and fulfilling life. By incorporating Zen principles into everyday routines, we create opportunities to reconnect with ourselves, our surroundings, and the present moment.

Through mindful eating, movement, and other rituals, we cultivate a sense of grounding that carries us through the complexities of modern life. These practices remind us that balance is not a distant goal but something we can nurture each day, one moment at a time.

As we explore the process of building long-term habits and balancing structure with flexibility in the following sections, the foundation of daily rituals will serve as a guiding thread—a reminder that the path to balance begins with small, intentional steps.

Building Long-Term Habits

Habits are the building blocks of our lives, shaping our days and ultimately defining who we become. In Zen, habits are not seen as mindless repetitions but as intentional practices that reflect our values and aspirations. By cultivating long-term habits aligned with Zen principles, we create a life of balance, mindfulness, and purpose. The process requires patience, awareness, and consistent effort, but the rewards are profound—a harmonious existence rooted in clarity and presence.

The Zen Approach to Habits

In Zen, habits are viewed through the lens of mindfulness. Each action, no matter how small, becomes an opportunity to embody the principles of presence and discipline. Unlike habits formed out of compulsion or convenience, Zen-inspired habits are deliberate choices, cultivated with care and intention.

The key to building long-term habits in Zen is consistency. Zen masters often emphasize the importance of showing up daily, even if the effort seems minimal. This philosophy is encapsulated in the Japanese concept of *kaizen*, or continuous improvement. *Kaizen* teaches that small, incremental changes lead to significant transformations over time. Whether sitting for a brief meditation each morning or taking a few mindful breaths during the day, these small acts accumulate, creating a foundation for sustainable growth.

Zen also recognizes the power of ritual in habit formation. By anchoring habits in meaningful rituals, we imbue them with a sense of purpose and connection. For example, lighting a candle before meditation or reciting a mantra before beginning a task transforms the habit into a sacred act, reinforcing its importance and deepening our commitment to it.

The Role of Awareness in Habit Formation

One of the most profound insights Zen offers is the importance of awareness in shaping habits. Many of our daily actions are performed on autopilot, driven by unconscious patterns rather than deliberate choices. Zen invites us to bring these patterns into the light of awareness, observing them with curiosity and compassion.

For instance, consider the habit of checking a smartphone first thing in the morning. This action, though seemingly trivial, sets the tone for the day, often leading to distraction and stress. By pausing to reflect on this habit, we can ask ourselves: Does this action align with my values? Does it contribute to my well-being? This process of inquiry helps us identify habits that no longer serve us and create space for more intentional choices.

Zen also teaches that awareness is essential for sustaining habits over the long term. By remaining attuned to the present moment, we can recognize when a habit begins to waver and gently guide ourselves back on track. This approach fosters resilience and self-compassion, allowing us to navigate setbacks without losing sight of our intentions.

Strategies for Building Consistency

Consistency is the cornerstone of habit formation, and Zen offers several strategies to cultivate it. One of the most effective is starting small.

Rather than attempting to overhaul one's life overnight, Zen encourages incremental changes that are manageable and sustainable. For example, committing to a five-minute meditation practice each day is more achievable—and ultimately more impactful—than attempting an hour-long session right away.

Another strategy is to create triggers or cues that remind us to practice our habits. In Zen monasteries, the ringing of a bell serves as a cue for meditation, signaling a return to mindfulness. In daily life, cues might include setting an alarm for a specific practice, placing a journal by the bedside to encourage evening reflection, or associating a habit with an existing routine, such as taking a mindful breath before starting a meal.

Accountability is also a powerful tool. Sharing our intentions with a friend, teacher, or community creates a sense of shared commitment, reinforcing our dedication to the habit. In Zen, this principle is reflected in the practice of *sangha*, or community, where practitioners support one another in their journey toward mindfulness and discipline.

The Power of Persistence and Patience

Building long-term habits is not without its challenges. There will be days when motivation wanes, distractions arise, or setbacks occur. Zen teaches that these moments are not failures but opportunities for growth. The practice of persistence—returning to the habit again and again, regardless of the obstacles—is what ultimately leads to mastery.

Zen master Shunryu Suzuki once said, "You are perfect just as you are, and you could use a little improvement." This paradox captures the essence of habit formation in Zen: accepting ourselves as we are while striving to embody our highest potential. By approaching habits with patience and self-compassion, we create an environment where growth becomes natural and sustainable.

It is also important to celebrate progress, no matter how small. In Zen, even the act of sitting for a single breath of meditation is seen as valuable. This perspective shifts the focus from outcomes to the process itself, fostering a sense of joy and fulfillment in the journey.

Transforming Habits into a Way of Being

Over time, habits cultivated with intention and mindfulness become more than actions—they become expressions of who we are. The Zen monk who sweeps the temple floor is not simply performing a task; they are embodying the principles of discipline, mindfulness, and service. Similarly, the habits we cultivate in daily life shape our character and influence how we engage with the world.

For example, a habit of mindful listening transforms our relationships, fostering deeper connections and mutual understanding. A habit of daily reflection strengthens our sense of purpose, guiding our decisions and actions. These habits, though seemingly small, ripple outward, creating a life that is aligned with our values and aspirations.

Conclusion: Habits as a Path to Freedom

In Zen, habits are not constraints but pathways

to freedom—a means of creating the conditions for balance, clarity, and inner peace. By approaching habit formation with mindfulness, consistency, and patience, we transform our daily actions into a practice of presence and purpose.

The journey of building long-term habits is not always linear, but it is always worthwhile. Each small step brings us closer to a life of harmony and fulfillment, a life where our actions reflect our deepest values. As we continue to explore the interplay between structure and flexibility in the next section, the habits we cultivate will serve as a foundation—a reminder that lasting change begins with the discipline of the present moment.

Balancing Structure with Flexibility

Discipline is the backbone of growth and mindfulness, but even the most carefully constructed routines must adapt to the unpredictability of life. In Zen, this balance between structure and flexibility is not a contradiction but a harmonious interplay. By cultivating the discipline to maintain structure and the wisdom to embrace

change, we create a life that is both grounded
and fluid—resilient in the face of challenges yet
open to the unexpected.

The Importance of Structure

Structure provides the foundation for discipline. It creates a framework that supports our
intentions, ensuring that our actions align with
our values and goals. In Zen, this principle is
embodied in the daily schedules of monastic life,
where periods of meditation, work, and rest are
carefully delineated. This structure is not about
rigidity but about creating space for presence
and mindfulness.

For example, the Zen practice of *zazen*, or seated
meditation, often takes place at the same time
each day. This consistency transforms the act
of sitting into a ritual, a reminder to return to
the present moment amidst the demands of life.
Similarly, the regularity of meals, work periods,
and shared practices in a Zen monastery fosters
a sense of rhythm and balance, anchoring the
mind and body.

In daily life, structure serves a similar purpose.

Whether it is a morning routine, a dedicated time for exercise, or a quiet moment of reflection before bed, these patterns create stability and predictability. They allow us to navigate the chaos of the world with greater ease, providing touchstones that keep us centered.

The Fluidity of Flexibility

While structure is essential, Zen also emphasizes the importance of flexibility—the ability to adapt to changing circumstances with grace and openness. This principle is rooted in the Zen teaching of impermanence, the understanding that all things are in a constant state of change. By embracing this reality, we learn to flow with life rather than resist it.

Consider the metaphor of water, often used in Zen to illustrate flexibility. Water takes the shape of its container, flows around obstacles, and adapts to the terrain without losing its essence. This fluidity is a reminder that true strength lies not in rigidity but in the ability to bend without breaking.

In practical terms, flexibility means recognizing

when to adjust our routines or let go of certain expectations. For instance, if a morning meditation practice is disrupted by an early meeting, a flexible approach might involve finding a few moments of mindfulness later in the day. This adaptability ensures that discipline remains a source of support rather than a source of stress.

The Interplay Between Structure and Flexibility

The balance between structure and flexibility is not about choosing one over the other but about integrating both. Zen teaches that these qualities are complementary, each enhancing the other. Structure provides the foundation for discipline, while flexibility allows us to sustain it in the face of life's uncertainties.

A clear example of this interplay can be found in the practice of mindful work. In a Zen monastery, work periods are structured and purposeful, yet the approach to each task is fluid and adaptable. Whether sweeping the floor, preparing a meal, or tending to the garden, practitioners respond to the needs of the moment, adjusting their actions with mindfulness and care.

In our own lives, we can cultivate this balance by creating routines that are both intentional and adaptable. For instance, a daily exercise routine might include a specific time and activity, such as a morning yoga session. However, if circumstances change—travel, illness, or unexpected commitments—a flexible approach might involve substituting the session with a brisk walk or a few stretches. This willingness to adjust ensures that the habit remains consistent while honoring the realities of the moment.

Overcoming Challenges to Balance

Finding the balance between structure and flexibility is not always easy. The demands of work, family, and societal expectations can create tension, pulling us toward extremes of rigidity or chaos. Zen offers practical guidance for navigating these challenges, emphasizing the importance of awareness and intention.

One of the most valuable tools is self-reflection. By regularly assessing our routines and habits, we can identify areas where structure may have become too rigid or where flexibility has given way to inconsistency. This process of reflection helps us make intentional adjustments, ensuring that our practices remain aligned with our values and goals.

Another strategy is to cultivate a sense of playfulness. Zen often uses humor and paradox to challenge rigid thinking, reminding us not to take ourselves too seriously. Approaching life with a spirit of curiosity and experimentation allows us to navigate changes with lightness and ease, transforming obstacles into opportunities for growth.

The Freedom Found in Balance

When structure and flexibility are in harmony, they create a sense of freedom. This freedom is not about doing whatever we want but about living with intention and responsiveness. It is the ability to maintain discipline without being confined by it, to adapt to change without losing our center.

Zen master Shunryu Suzuki captured this idea beautifully when he said, "To give your sheep or cow a large, spacious meadow is the way to control him." This paradoxical statement reflects the Zen understanding that freedom and discipline are not opposites but partners. By creating spaciousness within our routines, we allow ourselves to thrive.

For example, a writer might set aside a specific time each day for creative work, creating a structure that supports focus and productivity. Within that structure, however, there is room for exploration and spontaneity—allowing ideas to flow freely without the constraints of perfectionism. This balance fosters both consistency and inspiration, ensuring that the practice remains sustainable and fulfilling.

Conclusion: A Dynamic Practice

Balancing structure with flexibility is not a static achievement but a dynamic practice, one that evolves with the rhythms of life. It requires awareness, patience, and a willingness to experiment, but the rewards are profound—a life that is both grounded and free, disciplined and adaptable.

In Zen, this balance is not seen as an end in itself but as a means of cultivating presence and purpose. By integrating structure and flexibility into our routines, we create the conditions for mindfulness and growth, navigating the complexities of life with clarity and grace.

As we conclude this chapter, the interplay between structure and flexibility serves as a reminder that discipline is not about control but about alignment. It is the art of finding harmony within ourselves and with the world, creating a path that is both steady and responsive—a path that leads to balance, fulfillment, and inner peace.

CHAPTER 4: THE ART OF LETTING GO – EMBRACING CHANGE AND IMPERMANENCE

The Zen View of Impermanence

Impermanence is one of the most profound truths in Zen philosophy. Known as *mujo* in Japanese, it is the understanding that all things are transient, ever-changing, and in a constant state of flux. Far from being a source of despair, impermanence is celebrated in Zen as a gateway to freedom and a deeper appreciation of life's fleeting beauty. By embracing this truth, we learn to let go of attachments and live fully in the present moment.

The Beauty of Change

Zen finds beauty in impermanence, recognizing that the ephemeral nature of life gives it meaning. The cherry blossom, a beloved symbol in Japanese culture, embodies this philosophy. Its brief bloom, lasting only a few weeks, is a poignant reminder of life's transience. Yet, it is this very impermanence that makes the cherry blossom so cherished; its fleeting existence heightens our awareness of its delicate beauty.

This perspective encourages us to see change not as a loss but as a natural part of life's rhythm.

Just as the seasons transform from the vibrant greens of summer to the quiet stillness of winter, so too do our lives flow through cycles of growth, decay, and renewal. In embracing these cycles, we find a sense of harmony with the world around us.

The Teachings of the Buddha

The principle of impermanence lies at the heart of the Buddha's teachings. In his first sermon, the Buddha introduced the concept of the Four Noble Truths, which include the recognition that suffering arises from clinging to what is impermanent. Whether it is a relationship, a possession, or even our own identity, attachment to things that inevitably change leads to dissatisfaction and pain.

The Buddha's teaching on impermanence is not intended to be a source of fear but a path to liberation. By understanding that nothing is fixed or permanent, we can let go of the illusion of control and embrace life as it unfolds. This realization fosters a sense of equanimity, allowing us to navigate the highs and lows of existence with grace and acceptance.

Practical Lessons from Impermanence

In Zen practice, the awareness of impermanence is cultivated through mindfulness and meditation. Sitting in stillness, we observe the breath as it rises and falls, the thoughts as they come and go, and the sensations as they arise and fade. This practice helps us recognize the transient nature of our experiences, grounding us in the present moment.

One of the most profound lessons of impermanence is the reminder to cherish what we have while we have it. When we understand that everything is temporary, we are inspired to savor life's moments more deeply. A simple conversation with a loved one, the warmth of the sun on our skin, or the taste of a favorite meal becomes a precious experience when viewed through the lens of impermanence.

This awareness also helps us let go of unnecessary attachments. When we cling to something — whether a possession, a status, or a belief — we create suffering for ourselves. Zen teaches that by loosening our grip, we make space for new possibilities and experiences. Letting go is not about rejecting the world but about engaging with it more fully, free from the fear of loss.

Impermanence and Resilience

While impermanence reminds us of life's fragility, it also teaches us about resilience. Change, though often uncomfortable, is a source of growth and renewal. Just as a forest regenerates after a wildfire or a river carves its path through stone, we too have the capacity to adapt and thrive in the face of challenges.

Zen master Thích Nhất Hạnh once said, "Thanks to impermanence, everything is possible." This insight highlights the transformative power of change. When we release our attachment to how things "should" be, we open ourselves to the endless potential of what can be. This mindset fosters creativity, adaptability, and a profound sense of hope.

In practical terms, embracing impermanence helps us navigate life's inevitable transitions. Whether it is the end of a relationship, the loss of a job, or the passing of a loved one, the understanding that all things are temporary allows us to grieve without becoming consumed by sorrow. It also reminds us that every ending carries the seeds of a new beginning.

Finding Freedom in Letting Go

The Zen view of impermanence ultimately points us toward freedom. When we release our attachment to the idea of permanence, we free ourselves from the burden of trying to hold onto what cannot be held. This freedom is not about detachment in the sense of indifference but about engaging with life fully and wholeheartedly.

Consider the practice of creating a sand mandala, a ritual in Tibetan Buddhism that shares philosophical roots with Zen. Monks spend days or even weeks meticulously crafting intricate designs from colored sand, only to sweep them away upon completion. This ritual embodies the essence of impermanence, teaching that beauty and meaning exist not in permanence but in the act of creation itself.

In our own lives, we can embrace this principle by focusing on the journey rather than the destination. Whether pursuing a career, building a relationship, or exploring a passion, the joy lies in the process, not in the outcome. By letting go of the need for permanence, we free ourselves to experience life in all its richness and wonder.

Conclusion: The Gift of Impermanence

Impermanence is not a limitation but a gift—a reminder to live with presence, gratitude, and openness. It teaches us to cherish the fleeting moments that make up our lives, to let go of what no longer serves us, and to find beauty in the ever-changing flow of existence.

In embracing impermanence, we discover a profound sense of peace and resilience. We learn that change is not something to fear but something to celebrate—a natural and essential part of life's journey. As we continue to explore the art of letting go in the following sections, the Zen view of impermanence will serve as a guiding light, illuminating the path to freedom and fulfillment.

Letting Go of Attachments

Attachments often feel like anchors, tethering us to the people, possessions, and outcomes that we hold dear. Yet, in Zen, these attachments are seen not as sources of security but as obstacles to freedom and peace. Letting go does not mean rejecting the world or disengaging from relationships; rather, it is a practice of releasing the grip of expectation and control, allowing us to experience life with greater openness and ease.

The Nature of Attachment

Attachment arises from a natural desire to hold onto what we value, whether it be material possessions, loved ones, or aspirations. These connections can bring joy and meaning to our lives, but when we become overly attached, they can also lead to suffering. Zen teaches that clinging to anything—whether a fleeting moment of happiness or an unfulfilled desire—creates a cycle of longing and dissatisfaction, as nothing in life is permanent.

A poignant Zen story illustrates this principle. A monk carrying a treasured teacup was asked by a novice why he seemed so calm despite knowing the cup could break at any moment. The monk replied, "To me, the cup is already broken." This perspective reflects a deep understanding of impermanence: by accepting the eventual loss of the cup, the monk could cherish it without attachment, appreciating its beauty without fear of losing it.

This lesson can be extended to all aspects of life. Whether it is a cherished possession, a relationship, or a personal goal, the practice of letting go allows us to engage fully without becoming entangled. It is not about indifference but about cultivating a mindset of gratitude and acceptance.

Releasing Material Attachments

Material possessions often serve as symbols of security, status, or identity. However, the pursuit of more—more belongings, more luxury, more convenience—can become an endless cycle, leaving us feeling weighed down rather than enriched. Zen invites us to examine our relationship with material things, asking whether they truly serve us or whether we are serving them.

The practice of minimalism, inspired by Zen principles, offers a pathway to releasing material attachments. By decluttering our physical spaces, we create room for clarity and intention. This process is not about discarding for the sake of discarding but about mindfully evaluating what we truly need and value. Each item we let go of becomes an act of liberation, a step toward living more lightly.

For example, consider a person who has accumulated a wardrobe filled with clothes they no longer wear. By sorting through these items with care, keeping only those that spark joy or serve a purpose, they transform the act of decluttering into a practice of mindfulness. This same approach can be applied to other areas of life, from digital possessions to sentimental items, creating a sense of spaciousness that fosters peace and focus.

Navigating Attachments in Relationships

Letting go of attachments does not mean withdrawing from relationships or avoiding emotional bonds. On the contrary, Zen emphasizes the importance of deep and meaningful connections. However, it also teaches that clinging to relationships—whether out of fear, expectation, or dependency—can lead to suffering for both ourselves and others.

Healthy relationships are grounded in acceptance and mutual respect, free from the need to control or possess. Zen encourages us to approach relationships with the same mindset as the monk and his teacup: to cherish and honor them without trying to hold onto them too tightly. This perspective allows us to be fully present with the people in our lives, appreciating their unique qualities and supporting their growth.

For instance, a parent who clings to their child's childhood might struggle to accept the natural process of growing up, creating tension and resistance. By embracing change and letting go of expectations, the parent can cultivate a relationship that evolves with the child, fostering a deeper and more authentic connection.

Zen also invites us to practice detachment in conflict. When disagreements arise, the impulse to defend our perspective or "win" can escalate tension. By letting go of the need to be right, we create space for understanding and reconciliation. This approach not only strengthens relationships but also promotes inner peace.

Freeing Ourselves from Outcome Dependence

Attachment is not limited to possessions and relationships; it often extends to outcomes and goals. Whether pursuing a career ambition, planning a life event, or striving for personal growth, the desire for a specific result can create anxiety and frustration when reality does not align with our expectations.

Zen teaches that true freedom lies in focusing on the process rather than the outcome. This principle is reflected in the concept of *wu wei*, or effortless action, which encourages us to act with intention while releasing attachment to the result. By immersing ourselves fully in the present moment and trusting the natural flow of life, we find joy in the journey itself, regardless of where it leads.

A practical example of this principle can be found in creative endeavors. An artist who becomes fixated on creating a masterpiece may feel paralyzed by fear of failure, while one who paints for the sheer love of the process experiences freedom and fulfillment. This shift in perspective transforms effort into play, reducing stress and enhancing creativity.

The Practice of Letting Go

Letting go is not a one-time decision but an ongoing practice, a gentle untying of the knots that bind us to our attachments. Meditation and mindfulness provide powerful tools for this process, allowing us to observe our thoughts and feelings without judgment. By bringing awareness to our attachments, we can begin to loosen their grip, creating space for new possibilities.

One simple yet profound practice is the breath.

Each inhale and exhale is a reminder of life's rhythm of receiving and releasing. By focusing on the breath during moments of tension or clinging, we can anchor ourselves in the present and reconnect with the flow of life.

Gratitude also plays a vital role in letting go. By appreciating what we have without needing to possess it, we cultivate a sense of abundance and contentment. This mindset shifts our focus from what we lack to what we have, fostering a sense of peace and fulfillment.

Conclusion: A Path to Freedom

Letting go of attachments is not about giving up but about gaining freedom—freedom to live fully, love deeply, and embrace life as it is. By releasing our grip on possessions, relationships, and outcomes, we create space for joy, growth, and connection.

This practice is not always easy, but it is profoundly liberating. Each act of letting go brings us closer to the heart of Zen, where we discover that true security lies not in holding on but in letting be. As we continue to explore coping with loss and change in the next section, the art of releasing attachments will serve as a foundation—a reminder that in letting go, we gain everything.

Coping with Loss and Change

Loss is an inevitable part of life. Whether it comes in the form of a loved one's passing, the end of a relationship, or a significant life transition, it can leave us feeling unmoored and vulnerable. Zen, with its emphasis on impermanence and acceptance, offers profound wisdom for navigating these moments. By approaching loss with mindfulness and compassion, we can find healing and resilience, transforming pain into a source of growth and understanding.

Understanding Loss Through the Lens of Zen

In Zen, loss is not seen as an anomaly but as an integral part of life's natural cycle. The principle of *mujo*, or impermanence, teaches that everything we hold dear—people, possessions, experiences—will eventually change or fade away. While this truth can be difficult to accept, it also opens the door to a deeper appreciation of the present moment. Loss, as painful as it may be, reminds us to cherish the transient beauty of life.

One of the most poignant Zen teachings on loss comes from the concept of the "empty cup." In Zen, the cup is a metaphor for our expectations and attachments. When we hold onto these expectations too tightly, loss can shatter us, much like a cup breaking. However, when we approach life with an "empty cup" — open to whatever comes and goes — we create space for healing and renewal. This mindset helps us navigate loss with greater grace and acceptance.

The Role of Mindfulness in Grieving

Grief is a natural response to loss, but it often brings with it a whirlwind of emotions — sadness, anger, confusion, even guilt. Zen teaches that the first step in coping with grief is to allow ourselves to feel these emotions fully, without judgment or resistance. By sitting with our feelings and observing them with mindfulness, we create a space for healing to unfold.

Consider the practice of *zazen*, or seated meditation, as a tool for processing grief. In stillness, we can turn inward, acknowledging our pain without trying to fix or suppress it. Each breath becomes an anchor, grounding us in the present moment as we navigate the ebb and flow of emotions. Over time, this practice helps us build a sense of inner strength, allowing us to face loss with courage and compassion.

Mindfulness also encourages us to approach grief with curiosity rather than fear. Instead of asking, "Why did this happen to me?" we can ask, "What is this experience teaching me?" This shift in perspective transforms grief from a source of suffering into an opportunity for growth, deepening our understanding of ourselves and the world.

Finding Meaning in Loss

One of the most challenging aspects of loss is the sense of emptiness it leaves behind. Zen offers a pathway to finding meaning in this void, reminding us that every ending carries the seeds of a new beginning. By embracing impermanence, we learn to see loss not as a permanent state but as part of a larger process of transformation.

A powerful example of this principle can be found in the Zen practice of *ensō*, or drawing a circle. The circle, often left open at one point, symbolizes both completeness and the impermanence of all things. Just as the circle is never fully closed, loss is not an endpoint but a transition—a reminder that life is an ongoing journey of creation and renewal.

In practical terms, finding meaning in loss might involve creating a ritual to honor what has been lost. This could be as simple as lighting a candle, planting a tree, or writing a letter of gratitude. These acts of remembrance help us connect with the essence of what we have lost, transforming grief into a source of inspiration and connection.

Embracing Change as a Source of Growth

Loss often accompanies significant life changes—moving to a new city, changing careers, or entering a new stage of life. These transitions, while daunting, also offer opportunities for growth and reinvention. Zen teaches that by letting go of the past and embracing the uncertainty of change, we create space for new possibilities to emerge.

The story of the Zen master and the overflowing cup offers a valuable lesson in this regard. When a student came to the master seeking wisdom, the master began pouring tea into the student's cup until it overflowed. "Why do you continue pouring?" the student asked. The master replied, "You are like this cup—so full of your own assumptions that there is no room for anything new. Empty your cup, and then we can begin."

This story reminds us that letting go is not about forgetting but about making room for growth. By releasing our attachment to what was, we open ourselves to what can be, approaching change with curiosity and openness.

Practical Tools for Navigating Loss

Coping with loss requires not only mindfulness but also practical tools for self-care and support. One of the most powerful practices in Zen is the art of *metta*, or loving-kindness meditation. This practice involves sending thoughts of compassion and healing to oneself, others, and the world. By cultivating a sense of connection and kindness, *metta* helps to soften the edges of grief, providing comfort and solace.

Another practical tool is journaling. Writing down our thoughts and feelings creates a safe space for reflection and expression, allowing us to process our emotions at our own pace. Journaling can also help us identify patterns and insights, deepening our understanding of the loss and our journey through it.

Finally, seeking support from others is essential. In Zen, the concept of *sangha*, or community, emphasizes the importance of shared practice and connection. Whether through friends, family, or a support group, sharing our experiences with others helps to lighten the burden of grief, reminding us that we are not alone.

Conclusion: A Path to Healing

Loss and change are inevitable, but they need not define us. By approaching these experiences with mindfulness, compassion, and an openness to growth, we can navigate even the most challenging transitions with resilience and grace. Zen teaches that within every loss lies the potential for renewal, and within every change, the seeds of transformation.

As we continue to explore the art of letting go in the next section, the wisdom gained from coping with loss and change will serve as a foundation—a reminder that even in the face of impermanence, there is beauty, meaning, and the possibility of a brighter tomorrow.

The Freedom of Letting Go

To let go is to embrace freedom—a freedom that arises not from external circumstances but from within. In Zen, the act of releasing attachments, expectations, and the illusion of control opens the door to a life unburdened by fear and resistance. By fully accepting impermanence, we discover a profound sense of liberation, allowing us to live with authenticity, presence, and joy.

The Lightness of Being

Imagine carrying a heavy backpack filled with the burdens of attachment: the need for validation, the fear of change, the longing for things to remain as they are. With each step, the weight grows heavier, making the journey increasingly difficult. Now imagine setting the backpack down. The simple act of letting go brings an immediate sense of relief, lightness, and clarity.

This metaphor captures the essence of letting go. When we release our attachments, we free ourselves from the weight of expectations and desires that no longer serve us. This freedom is not about abandoning responsibility or disengaging from life but about living with greater intention and ease.

Zen master Shunryu Suzuki once said, "When you let go, everything gets done." This paradox highlights the transformative power of letting go: by relinquishing control, we allow life to unfold naturally, aligning ourselves with its flow. This state of openness and acceptance is the foundation of true freedom.

Living in the Present

Letting go enables us to live fully in the present moment, unencumbered by regrets about the past or anxieties about the future. Zen teaches that the present is the only moment that truly exists, the only space where life can be experienced and appreciated. By letting go of what was and what might be, we create the conditions for a more vibrant and meaningful existence.

Consider the Zen practice of mindful walking. With each step, the practitioner focuses on the sensation of the feet touching the ground, the rhythm of the breath, and the sounds of the environment. There is no rush, no destination, only the experience of walking itself. This practice exemplifies the freedom that comes from letting go of distractions and immersing oneself fully in the present.

In daily life, this principle can be applied to even the simplest activities, such as drinking a cup of tea or having a conversation. By releasing the need to multitask or achieve a specific outcome, we bring our full attention to the moment, transforming ordinary experiences into extraordinary ones.

The Courage to Let Go

Letting go requires courage, as it often involves

stepping into the unknown. Whether releasing a long-held belief, ending a relationship, or pursuing a new path, the act of letting go challenges us to confront our fears and trust in the process of life. Yet, it is in these moments of vulnerability that we discover our greatest strength.

The story of the Zen archer illustrates this courage. In traditional Zen archery, the goal is not to hit the target but to let go of the arrow with complete presence and intention. The archer practices for years, not to perfect their aim but to perfect the art of releasing the arrow without attachment to the result. This practice mirrors the process of letting go in life: it is not about controlling the outcome but about fully committing to the moment of release.

For many, the courage to let go is cultivated through mindfulness and self-compassion. By observing our fears and doubts without judgment, we create a safe space to explore and embrace change. This process helps us build the resilience needed to face life's uncertainties with grace and confidence.

The Joy of Detachment

Zen detachment is not about withdrawing from life but about engaging with it more deeply and authentically. By letting go of our attachment to outcomes, we free ourselves to explore, create, and connect without fear of failure or loss. This sense of detachment fosters a profound joy, a recognition that life's beauty lies not in its permanence but in its impermanence.

Consider the practice of creating a sand mandala, a ritual in Tibetan Buddhism that shares philosophical roots with Zen. Monks spend days or weeks crafting intricate designs from colored sand, only to sweep them away upon completion. This ritual embodies the joy of detachment, celebrating the process of creation rather than the permanence of the result.

In our own lives, we can cultivate this joy by focusing on the journey rather than the destination. Whether pursuing a creative project, building a relationship, or exploring a passion, the act of engaging fully in the present moment becomes its own reward. This shift in perspective transforms challenges into opportunities, fostering a sense of curiosity and wonder.

The Ripple Effect of Freedom

Letting go not only transforms our inner experience but also ripples outward, influencing our relationships and interactions with the world. When we release our need to control others, we create space for genuine connection and mutual respect. When we let go of rigid expectations, we open ourselves to new possibilities and perspectives.

This ripple effect is evident in the Zen concept of *interbeing*, the understanding that all things are interconnected. By letting go of our individual attachments, we contribute to the harmony of the larger whole, fostering a sense of unity and compassion. This perspective reminds us that freedom is not a solitary endeavor but a shared experience, one that enriches both ourselves and the world around us.

Conclusion: A Life Liberated

The freedom of letting go is not about escaping life but about embracing it fully, with all its beauty and impermanence. It is the liberation that comes from releasing the need to hold on, the joy of living with openness and intention. Zen teaches that in letting go, we find not emptiness but fullness—a life unburdened by fear, rich with presence, and aligned with the natural flow of existence.

As we conclude this chapter, the art of letting go serves as a guiding principle for navigating life's complexities. By embracing impermanence, we discover a profound sense of freedom and fulfillment, a reminder that the greatest gift we can give ourselves is the courage to release and the grace to accept.

CHAPTER 5: INNER PEACE THROUGH SIMPLICITY – DECLUTTERING THE MIND AND LIFE

The Zen Aesthetic of Simplicity

Simplicity is at the heart of Zen. From the quiet elegance of a rock garden to the understated beauty of a tea ceremony, Zen aesthetics reflect a profound appreciation for the minimal and the essential. This philosophy, rooted in centuries of practice, reveals that simplicity is not merely an absence of excess but a deliberate choice to focus on what truly matters. By embracing the Zen aesthetic of simplicity, we cultivate a sense of clarity and peace that extends beyond our physical surroundings to the mind and spirit.

The Essence of Zen Minimalism

Zen minimalism is not about stripping life to its bare bones for the sake of austerity. Instead, it is about finding harmony through balance and purpose. Each element in a Zen-inspired space serves a specific function, and each function contributes to a sense of tranquility and presence. The Japanese term *wabi-sabi* captures this perspective, celebrating the beauty of imperfection, impermanence, and authenticity.

A Zen garden, for instance, may consist of nothing more than raked gravel, a few rocks, and sparse greenery. Yet, this simplicity invites reflection and fosters a deep connection to nature. The empty spaces in the garden are as significant as the elements within it, symbolizing the importance of what is not there as much as what is. This interplay between form and emptiness encourages mindfulness, inviting us to appreciate the subtle details that often go unnoticed in more cluttered environments.

The Influence of Zen on Design

The principles of Zen have inspired design movements around the world, from traditional Japanese interiors to modern minimalism. The clean lines, neutral colors, and open spaces characteristic of Zen design create an atmosphere of calm and focus, reflecting the philosophy's emphasis on simplicity and balance.

One of the most iconic examples of Zen-inspired design is the *tatami* room, a traditional Japanese living space. With its tatami mats, sliding paper doors, and sparse furnishings, the room embodies the Zen aesthetic. Each element is carefully chosen for its functionality and beauty, creating a space that feels both serene and intentional. The simplicity of the *tatami* room not only reduces visual noise but also fosters a sense of humility and mindfulness.

In contemporary design, these principles are often adapted to create spaces that prioritize comfort and clarity. For example, a minimalist workspace with clean surfaces and a few carefully chosen decorations can enhance productivity and reduce stress. Similarly, a decluttered living room with soft lighting and natural materials creates an environment conducive to relaxation and connection.

The Connection Between Simplicity and Mental Clarity

Zen teaches that our external environment reflects and influences our internal state. A cluttered space often mirrors a cluttered mind, filled with distractions and unresolved thoughts. Conversely, a simple and harmonious space fosters mental clarity, creating the conditions for focus, creativity, and peace.

This connection between simplicity and mental clarity is supported by modern psychology. Studies have shown that cluttered environments can increase stress levels and decrease productivity, while minimalist spaces promote a sense of order and well-being. By reducing physical distractions, we create room for mental stillness, allowing us to engage more fully with the present moment.

Consider the practice of sitting meditation, or *zazen*. In a Zen meditation hall, the design is intentionally minimal, with plain walls, natural materials, and sparse decorations. This simplicity eliminates distractions, directing the practitioner's attention inward. The same principle can be applied to our daily lives: by simplifying our surroundings, we create a sanctuary for the mind, a space where we can think, feel, and be with greater clarity.

Practical Applications of Zen Simplicity

Embracing the Zen aesthetic of simplicity does not require a complete overhaul of our living spaces. Instead, it begins with small, intentional changes that align with our values and needs. For example, removing unnecessary items from a desk can transform it into a space for focused work. Similarly, choosing furnishings and decorations that evoke a sense of calm—such as neutral colors, natural materials, and meaningful objects—can create an atmosphere of serenity.

Zen also encourages us to consider the flow and purpose of our spaces. In a kitchen, for instance, simplicity might involve organizing tools and ingredients for efficiency and ease, allowing the act of cooking to become a mindful ritual. In a bedroom, simplicity might mean prioritizing comfort and removing distractions, creating a space dedicated to rest and renewal.

These changes are not about achieving a specific aesthetic but about cultivating a sense of harmony and intention. By simplifying our surroundings, we create the conditions for a more mindful and fulfilling life.

The Philosophy Behind the Aesthetic

At its core, the Zen aesthetic of simplicity is not about the material but the spiritual. It is a reminder to focus on what is essential, to let go of what distracts or burdens us, and to find beauty in the ordinary. This philosophy extends beyond design to all aspects of life, encouraging us to approach each moment with intention and presence.

The Zen poet Ryōkan captured this perspective in his simple yet profound verse:
"How happy we are,
living without possessions!
Even the morning dew is more than we need."

These words reflect the joy and freedom that come from embracing simplicity, from realizing that contentment does not come from accumulation but from appreciating the abundance already present in our lives.

Conclusion: Simplicity as a Path to Peace

The Zen aesthetic of simplicity offers more than just a design philosophy; it is a way of life. By focusing on the essential, we create spaces and experiences that nurture clarity, presence, and peace. This simplicity is not about deprivation but about liberation—a release from the noise and excess that distract us from what truly matters.

As we continue to explore the principles of simplicity in the following sections, the Zen aesthetic serves as a foundation, guiding us toward a life that is not only more beautiful but also more meaningful. In embracing simplicity, we discover that less is not just more—it is everything.

Decluttering Your Physical Space

In the Zen tradition, the physical environment is viewed as an extension of the mind. A cluttered space can mirror a cluttered psyche, while a clean, minimalist environment fosters clarity and peace. Decluttering, therefore, is not just an act of tidying up; it is a practice of creating harmony and intention in our surroundings. By letting go of excess and organizing what remains, we transform our homes and workplaces into sanctuaries of calm and mindfulness.

The Philosophy of Decluttering in Zen

Zen approaches decluttering with the same mindfulness and purpose that it brings to all practices. This is not about achieving a sterile or overly sparse aesthetic but about fostering a sense of balance and flow. Each item in a Zen-inspired space is chosen with care, serving a functional or meaningful purpose. The absence of excess creates a sense of openness and freedom, allowing the mind to rest.

One of the guiding principles of Zen decluttering is *ma*, a Japanese concept that refers to the space between things. *Ma* emphasizes the importance of emptiness, suggesting that the spaces we leave unfilled are just as valuable as the objects we choose to include. A room with *ma* feels spacious and inviting, offering room for thought, movement, and presence.

The Emotional Weight of Clutter

Clutter is more than a physical obstacle; it often carries an emotional weight. Each object we keep can represent an unfulfilled promise, an unresolved decision, or a past we struggle to let go of. A stack of unread books might remind us of ambitions unmet, while a closet full of unworn clothes might evoke feelings of guilt or indecision.

Zen teaches that holding onto these items can drain our energy, tying us to the past or projecting us into an imagined future. By decluttering, we release these burdens and create space for the present. This act of letting go is not about discarding carelessly but about making intentional choices that align with our values and aspirations.

The Process of Decluttering

Decluttering begins with mindfulness. Before deciding what to keep or discard, it is helpful to take a moment to reflect on the purpose of the space. What do you want it to feel like? What activities will it support? These questions provide a foundation for making choices that are both practical and meaningful.

One effective method is to approach the process in stages, starting with a single room or category of items. For example, you might begin with your wardrobe, evaluating each piece of clothing based on its utility and the joy it brings. Holding each item in your hands, as Zen practitioners suggest, helps to cultivate awareness and intention. This practice not only simplifies the process but also deepens your connection to the items you choose to keep.

Another key principle is to focus on what to keep rather than what to discard. This shift in perspective encourages gratitude and mindfulness, allowing you to prioritize the items that truly matter. For instance, in a kitchen, you might choose to keep only the tools and ingredients that inspire creativity and ease in cooking, letting go of duplicates or unused gadgets.

Creating a Calming Environment

A decluttered space is not just about reducing physical objects; it is about creating an environment that supports calm and focus. In Zen design, natural elements like wood, stone, and plants are often incorporated to foster a sense of connection with nature. Soft, neutral colors and simple textures create a soothing backdrop, while natural light enhances the feeling of openness.

In practice, creating a calming environment

might involve rearranging furniture to improve the flow of the room, adding a plant to bring life and vitality, or introducing soft lighting to create a warm and inviting atmosphere. These small changes can have a profound impact, transforming a space from chaotic to tranquil.

Consider the example of a Zen tea room. These spaces are intentionally minimal, often featuring a single flower arrangement, a tea set, and a scroll with a calligraphic inscription. This simplicity invites the mind to settle, allowing those who enter to focus fully on the act of making and drinking tea. While a modern home or office might serve different functions, the principles of simplicity and intention can be applied to create a similarly calming effect.

The Ripple Effect of Decluttering

The benefits of decluttering extend far beyond the physical space. As we simplify our surroundings, we often find that our minds become clearer and our priorities more focused. The act of letting go fosters a sense of empowerment and renewal, breaking the cycle of accumulation and creating room for new possibilities.

This ripple effect is evident in the stories of those who have embraced minimalist living. Many report feeling a greater sense of freedom and creativity, as well as improved relationships and well-being. By reducing distractions, they are able to dedicate more time and energy to what truly matters—whether it is pursuing a passion, spending time with loved ones, or simply enjoying the present moment.

Zen master Thích Nhất Hạnh captures this sentiment beautifully: "Smile, breathe, and go slowly." These simple words remind us that the process of decluttering is not a race but a mindful journey, one that can transform not only our spaces but also our lives.

Sustaining Simplicity

Decluttering is not a one-time event but an ongoing practice. As life evolves, new items will inevitably enter our spaces, and old ones will lose their relevance. Zen teaches us to approach this process with mindfulness, regularly reassessing our surroundings and making adjustments as needed.

One way to sustain simplicity is to adopt a mindset of intentionality. Before bringing something new into your space, consider whether it aligns with your values and serves a meaningful purpose. This practice helps to prevent clutter from accumulating and reinforces the sense of clarity and balance you have worked to create.

Another practice is to cultivate gratitude for the items you choose to keep. By appreciating their presence and purpose, you strengthen your connection to your space and the life it supports. This gratitude fosters a sense of contentment, reducing the desire for more and deepening your appreciation for what already is.

Conclusion: A Path to Inner Peace

Decluttering your physical space is more than an act of organization; it is a path to inner peace. By creating an environment that reflects the principles of Zen simplicity, you foster a sense of clarity, balance, and intention that extends to every aspect of your life. This process is not about perfection but about presence—a mindful journey toward a space that nurtures and inspires.

As we continue to explore the principles of simplicity in the following sections, the act of decluttering serves as a foundation, reminding us that the path to peace begins with letting go. Through this practice, we discover that simplicity is not about what we remove but about what we make space for—a life of purpose, connection, and joy.

Simplifying Mental Overload

In a world filled with constant stimulation, information, and demands, the mind can easily become a crowded and chaotic space. Just as a cluttered physical environment can drain our energy, a cluttered mind can leave us feeling overwhelmed and unbalanced. Simplifying mental overload is not about ignoring responsibilities or disengaging from life; it is about cultivating clarity and focus through intentional practices. By reducing mental clutter, we free our minds to be more present, creative, and resilient.

The Nature of Mental Clutter

Mental clutter often arises from the relentless flow of thoughts, worries, and distractions that compete for our attention. It may take the form of unprocessed emotions, unresolved tasks, or an endless loop of "what if" scenarios. Zen teaches that this clutter is not an inherent part of the mind but a byproduct of attachment—our tendency to hold onto thoughts and expectations rather than letting them pass.

The Zen practice of *zazen*, or seated meditation, offers a powerful metaphor for understanding mental clutter. During meditation, thoughts inevitably arise, but the goal is not to suppress or control them. Instead, practitioners are encouraged to observe their thoughts like clouds drifting across the sky, acknowledging their presence without becoming entangled. This practice teaches us that mental clarity is not about eliminating thoughts but about creating space for them to come and go.

The Power of Awareness

Simplifying mental overload begins with awareness. By paying attention to the patterns of our thoughts and the sources of our stress, we can identify what contributes to our mental clutter. This process is not about judging or criticizing ourselves but about approaching our minds with curiosity and compassion.

One effective way to cultivate awareness is through mindfulness meditation. By setting aside a few minutes each day to focus on the breath or a specific sensation, we train our minds to stay present and grounded. Over time, this practice helps us recognize when our thoughts are spiraling and gently redirect our attention to the present moment.

Another tool for building awareness is journaling. Writing down our thoughts and emotions provides a safe space to process and reflect, allowing us to externalize what might otherwise feel overwhelming. Journaling can also help us identify recurring themes or concerns, offering valuable insights into our mental habits.

The Practice of Prioritization

One of the most common sources of mental overload is the sheer volume of tasks and commitments we juggle on a daily basis. Zen offers a simple yet profound solution: focus on what is essential. This principle aligns with the Japanese concept of *ichigyo-zammai*, or "one act at a time," which emphasizes giving full attention to the task at hand.

Prioritization is not just about managing tasks but about aligning them with our values and goals. By identifying what truly matters, we can let go of distractions and delegate or decline what does not serve our purpose. This process creates space for deeper engagement and reduces the mental strain of trying to do it all.

A practical approach to prioritization is to begin each day by identifying one or two key tasks that will have the greatest impact. These tasks become the focus of our attention, allowing us to approach them with clarity and intention. At the same time, we can practice letting go of the need for perfection, recognizing that progress is more important than achieving an ideal outcome.

Techniques for Mental Simplification

Zen offers a variety of techniques for reducing mental clutter and cultivating clarity. One such practice is *shoshin*, or "beginner's mind." This mindset encourages us to approach each moment with openness and curiosity, free from preconceived notions or judgments. By adopting a beginner's mind, we can break free from habitual thinking patterns and see situations with fresh perspective.

Another technique is to create mental boundaries through mindful transitions. For example, taking a few deep breaths before starting a new task or setting aside time to reflect at the end of the day can help us compartmentalize our thoughts and prevent them from bleeding into unrelated areas of our lives. These boundaries create a sense of order and flow, reducing the mental chaos that often accompanies multitasking.

Zen also emphasizes the importance of pausing. In a culture that values constant productivity, taking moments of stillness may feel counterintuitive, but these pauses are essential for mental clarity. Whether it is a short meditation, a walk in nature, or simply closing our eyes and breathing deeply, these moments of rest allow the mind to reset and recharge.

The Role of Simplified Communication

Mental clutter is not limited to our internal thoughts; it is often compounded by the demands of modern communication—emails, messages, notifications, and social media. Zen invites us to simplify these interactions by approaching them with intention and mindfulness.

One way to simplify communication is to set boundaries around technology use. For instance, designating specific times for checking emails or turning off notifications during focused work periods can reduce the constant pull of digital distractions. These boundaries help us stay present and prevent the fragmented attention that contributes to mental overload.

Zen also encourages us to practice mindful communication. By listening fully and speaking with clarity and purpose, we create meaningful connections and reduce misunderstandings. This practice not only simplifies interactions but also fosters a sense of harmony and respect in our relationships.

The Freedom Found in Mental Clarity

As we simplify our mental landscape, we begin to experience a profound sense of freedom. This freedom is not about having fewer responsibilities but about approaching life with a clear and focused mind. It allows us to be more present with ourselves and others, to make decisions with confidence, and to respond to challenges with resilience.

The Zen poet Ryōkan captured this freedom in his writings:
"In my hut this spring,
there is nothing—
there is everything."
These words remind us that clarity is not about

emptiness but about fullness—the fullness of being fully alive in the moment.

Conclusion: A Clearer Mind, A Fuller Life

Simplifying mental overload is a journey of mindfulness and intention. By cultivating awareness, prioritizing what matters, and creating boundaries around our thoughts and interactions, we free our minds to focus on what is truly meaningful. This process is not about perfection but about presence, a reminder that clarity begins with small, intentional steps.

As we move into the next section, celebrating the joy of living simply, the practices of simplifying mental clutter provide a foundation for a life that is both peaceful and purposeful. Through this journey, we discover that the greatest gift we can give ourselves is the space to think, feel, and be with clarity and ease.

The Joy of Living Simply

Simplicity is more than an aesthetic choice or a practical approach to life—it is a state of being that nurtures peace, contentment, and fulfillment. In Zen, the joy of living simply comes not from what we lack but from what we gain: clarity, presence, and the freedom to engage fully with the richness of the present moment. By embracing simplicity, we create space for what truly matters, rediscovering the profound beauty in the ordinary.

The Essence of Joy in Simplicity

In a world driven by the pursuit of more—more possessions, achievements, and experiences—the Zen approach offers a counterpoint: finding joy in less. This philosophy is not about deprivation but about alignment, choosing what resonates with our values and letting go of what does not. When we release the unnecessary, we uncover the treasures hidden in simplicity.

Consider the Zen tradition of the tea ceremony. At first glance, the ritual appears simple—boiling water, preparing tea, and sharing it with others. Yet, within this simplicity lies a profound depth. Every gesture, from the placement of the teapot to the way the tea is poured, is performed with mindfulness and intention. This focus transforms a routine act into a moment of connection and gratitude, exemplifying the joy that arises from living simply.

Simplicity as a Path to Freedom

Living simply frees us from the weight of unnecessary burdens. Material possessions, constant busyness, and unexamined expectations can tether us, limiting our ability to move through life with ease and flexibility. By simplifying, we reclaim our energy and attention, redirecting them toward the things that bring genuine fulfillment.

One Zen teaching illustrates this freedom through the image of a monk traveling with a single bowl. Carrying only what is essential, the monk moves lightly through the world, unencumbered by excess. This metaphor reminds us that simplicity is not about what we have but about how we carry it—choosing to lighten our load and focus on what truly sustains us.

In modern life, this freedom might take the form of decluttering our schedules to make time for meaningful activities, letting go of possessions that no longer serve us, or releasing the pressure

to meet others' expectations. Each act of simplification is a step toward liberation, allowing us
to live with greater intention and authenticity.

The Richness of the Present Moment

Simplicity creates the conditions for presence,
allowing us to fully engage with the here and
now. When our surroundings and minds are
free from clutter, we can focus on the details
that often go unnoticed—the warmth of the sun
on our skin, the sound of birdsong, the taste of
a home-cooked meal. These moments, though
fleeting, are the essence of life, and simplicity
helps us to savor them.

Zen emphasizes the importance of slowing
down and appreciating these simple joys. The
practice of mindful walking, for example, transforms an everyday activity into an opportunity
for reflection and connection. With each step,
the practitioner becomes attuned to the rhythm
of their breath, the texture of the ground beneath their feet, and the beauty of the world
around them. This mindfulness fosters a sense
of gratitude, turning ordinary moments into

extraordinary experiences.

In our daily lives, we can cultivate this presence by simplifying our routines and setting aside time for stillness. Whether it is a quiet morning with a cup of tea or an evening spent watching the sunset, these moments of simplicity remind us of the abundance that exists in the present moment.

The Role of Gratitude in Simplicity

Gratitude is both a byproduct and a catalyst of living simply. When we strip away distractions and excess, we gain a clearer view of what truly enriches our lives—our relationships, passions, and the natural world. This awareness deepens our appreciation for what we have, fostering a sense of contentment and peace.

Zen poetry often captures this gratitude in its reflections on nature and daily life. The 17th-century poet Matsuo Bashō, for instance, wrote:
"An old silent pond...
A frog jumps into the pond—
Splash! Silence again."
In these few words, Bashō invites us to find joy

in the simplicity of a single moment, a reminder that beauty and meaning are always within reach.

Practicing gratitude in our own lives can take many forms. Writing in a journal, expressing appreciation to loved ones, or simply pausing to reflect on the good in our lives are all ways to nurture this mindset. Gratitude shifts our focus from what we lack to what we have, reinforcing the joy that comes from living simply.

Simplicity in Relationships

The joy of simplicity extends to our relationships, where it fosters authenticity and connection. When we let go of the need to impress or control others, we create space for genuine interactions based on mutual respect and understanding. This simplicity deepens our bonds, allowing us to be fully present with those we care about.

Zen encourages us to approach relationships with the same mindfulness and intention that we bring to other aspects of life. Listening fully, speaking with clarity, and being attentive to the needs of others are all ways to embody simplicity in our interactions. These practices strengthen our connections and remind us that relationships thrive not on complexity but on presence and care.

The Enduring Peace of a Simple Life

Living simply is not a destination but an ongoing practice, a journey of continually refining and realigning our lives with what matters most. It is a path that offers enduring peace, teaching us that contentment is not found in accumulation but in appreciation.

This peace is evident in the story of Ryōkan, a Zen monk known for his humble and joyful life. Legend has it that one night, a thief broke into Ryōkan's hut, only to find that there was nothing to steal. Instead of reacting with anger, Ryōkan wrote a poem:
"The thief left it behind—
the moon at my window."
These words reflect a deep sense of freedom and gratitude, a reminder that even in the simplest of

circumstances, there is beauty and abundance.

Conclusion: The Joy of Letting Go

The joy of living simply lies not in what we lack but in what we gain—a life of clarity, presence, and connection. By embracing simplicity, we free ourselves from the distractions and burdens that cloud our vision, allowing us to see and appreciate the richness of the present moment.

As we conclude this chapter, the principles of simplicity serve as a foundation for inner peace and fulfillment. They remind us that the path to joy is not found in chasing more but in cherishing less, in finding beauty in the ordinary and meaning in the essential. Through simplicity, we discover a life that is both lighter and fuller, a life that nurtures the heart and soul.

CHAPTER 6: HARMONY IN RELATIONSHIPS – PRACTICING ZEN WITH OTHERS

The Role of Compassion in Zen

Compassion lies at the heart of Zen practice. It is more than a feeling or an action—it is a way of being that permeates how we interact with ourselves, others, and the world. In relationships, compassion serves as a bridge, connecting us through understanding, empathy, and a shared humanity. By embracing the Zen approach to compassion, we nurture the bonds that sustain us, creating harmony and depth in our connections.

The Zen Philosophy of Compassion

In Zen, compassion is rooted in the principle of *karuna*, which translates to an active desire to alleviate suffering and promote well-being. This principle is not limited to grand gestures but is expressed in small, everyday acts of kindness and presence. Compassion, in this sense, is not something we give or receive but something we embody, reflecting a deep awareness of our interconnectedness.

The Zen teaching of *interbeing*, popularized by Thích Nhất Hạnh, emphasizes this interconnectedness. It suggests that our existence is intertwined with the lives of others, and that the well-being of one is inseparable from the well-being of all. When we approach relationships with this understanding, compassion becomes a natural response—a recognition that another's pain is also our own, and their joy is a shared experience.

Historical Teachings on Compassion

The story of Avalokiteshvara, the Bodhisattva of Compassion, provides a powerful metaphor for the role of compassion in Zen. According to legend, Avalokiteshvara vowed to free all beings from suffering. Yet, overwhelmed by the enormity of this task, he cried out in despair. His head split into pieces, but through his practice, each piece transformed into a new face, allowing him to see and respond to the needs of all beings. His hands multiplied as well, enabling him to reach out in countless ways.

This story illustrates that compassion is not about solving every problem or carrying the weight of the world alone. Instead, it is about cultivating the capacity to be present with others' experiences and to act from a place of love and care, even in the face of challenges. It also reminds us that compassion is not a finite resource—it expands as we practice it, enriching both ourselves and those around us.

Cultivating Empathy Through Presence

At the core of compassion is empathy—the ability to understand and share the feelings of another. Zen teaches that empathy arises naturally when we are fully present. By quieting our own thoughts and judgments, we create space to truly listen and connect with the experiences of others.

One of the most profound practices for cultivating empathy is mindful observation. In Zen, this involves paying close attention to another person's words, expressions, and emotions without imposing our own interpretations or solutions. This kind of presence communicates a deep respect and care, fostering trust and understanding.

For example, consider a conversation with a friend who is experiencing difficulty. Rather than offering advice or shifting the focus to our own experiences, we might simply listen with an open heart, acknowledging their pain and allowing them to feel seen and heard. This simple act of presence can be transformative, both for the person receiving compassion and for the one offering it.

The Practice of Self-Compassion

Compassion is not only something we extend to others; it must also begin with ourselves. Zen emphasizes that self-compassion is the foundation for authentic and sustainable relationships. When we treat ourselves with kindness and understanding, we create the inner resources needed to support and care for others.

Self-compassion involves recognizing our own struggles and imperfections without judgment. Instead of criticizing ourselves for perceived shortcomings, we can approach them with curiosity and acceptance, asking, "What can I learn from this experience?" This shift in perspective fosters resilience and self-awareness, allowing us to navigate challenges with greater ease.

In practice, self-compassion might involve taking a moment to breathe deeply during a stressful day, forgiving ourselves for a mistake, or seeking support when needed. These acts of kindness toward ourselves create a ripple effect, enabling us to approach others with greater patience and empathy.

Compassion in Action

Compassion is not just a state of mind but a practice that is expressed through our actions. Zen encourages us to look for opportunities to ease the suffering of others, whether through small acts of kindness, words of encouragement, or simply being present. These actions do not need to be dramatic or self-sacrificing; even the smallest gesture can have a profound impact.

Consider the Zen teaching of *dana*, or generosity. This practice involves giving freely and without expectation, whether it is offering time, resources, or attention. In relationships, *dana* might manifest as helping a neighbor, supporting a colleague, or making time for a loved one. These acts of generosity deepen our connections and remind us of the abundance that comes from sharing.

Compassion also involves recognizing and honoring boundaries—both our own and others'. Zen teaches that true compassion does not mean overextending ourselves or enabling harmful behaviors. Instead, it involves acting with integrity and respect, balancing care with wisdom.

The Transformative Power of Compassion

When practiced consistently, compassion transforms not only our relationships but also our own sense of purpose and well-being. It shifts our focus from individual concerns to the larger web of connection, fostering a sense of belonging and meaning. This transformation is evident in the lives of Zen practitioners who have dedicated themselves to serving others, from monks tending to their communities to lay practitioners offering mindfulness in schools and hospitals.

Compassion also has the power to heal conflicts and divisions. By approaching disagreements with empathy and understanding, we can bridge gaps and find common ground. This approach does not mean ignoring differences but embracing them as opportunities for growth and connection.

Conclusion: A Foundation for Harmony

Compassion is the cornerstone of harmonious relationships, offering a path to deeper connection and mutual understanding. By cultivating empathy, practicing self-compassion, and expressing care through our actions, we create a foundation for meaningful and fulfilling interactions. Zen reminds us that compassion is not a finite resource but a practice that grows and expands with intention, enriching every aspect of our lives.

As we continue to explore the principles of mindful communication in the next section, the role of compassion serves as a guiding light—a reminder that true connection begins with the simple act of being present, both with ourselves and with others.

Mindful Communication

In Zen, communication is viewed not simply as the exchange of words but as an opportunity for connection, understanding, and presence. Mindful communication transforms ordinary conversations into meaningful interactions, fostering harmony and respect in relationships. By approaching dialogue with intention and awareness, we create a space where both we and others can feel seen, heard, and valued.

The Foundation of Mindful Communication

At its core, mindful communication is rooted in two Zen principles: awareness and intention. Awareness involves being fully present in the moment, attuned to the words, emotions, and needs of ourselves and others. Intention, on the other hand, focuses on the purpose behind our words—whether we seek to inform, support, or connect. When combined, these principles create a foundation for dialogue that is both authentic and compassionate.

One of the central teachings of Zen communication is the concept of *right speech*, a principle from the Buddha's Noble Eightfold Path. *Right speech* emphasizes speaking truthfully, kindly, and with purpose. It encourages us to consider the impact of our words before we speak, asking whether they are necessary, helpful, and aligned with our values.

The Art of Active Listening

Active listening is a cornerstone of mindful communication. In Zen, listening is more than hearing words; it is an act of presence and empathy. By giving our full attention to the speaker, we create a sense of trust and understanding that deepens the connection between us.

To practice active listening, Zen encourages us to approach conversations with a "beginner's mind." This means setting aside assumptions, judgments, and distractions, and approaching the speaker's words with openness and curiosity. For example, when a friend shares their thoughts, we might focus not only on their words but also on their tone, body language, and underlying emotions. This attentiveness allows us to respond with greater insight and care.

One Zen story illustrates the power of listening: A student asked their master, "What is the essence of Zen?" The master replied, "When I eat, I eat. When I listen, I listen." This simple response underscores the importance of being fully present in each moment, whether it is a meal or a conversation. By practicing this level of presence in our interactions, we honor both the speaker and the act of communication itself.

Mindfulness in Speaking

Mindful communication also involves speaking with awareness and intention. In Zen, this practice begins with pausing—a brief moment to reflect before responding. This pause creates space to consider our words and their potential impact, ensuring that what we say aligns with our intentions.

Zen teachings emphasize the importance of speaking with clarity and simplicity. In a culture that often values verbosity, Zen encourages us to distill our thoughts into words that are precise and meaningful. This simplicity not only

enhances understanding but also reduces the
risk of miscommunication.

For example, a manager addressing a team
might focus on providing clear and concise instructions, accompanied by expressions of appreciation and encouragement. This approach
not only conveys the necessary information
but also fosters a sense of mutual respect and
motivation.

Navigating Difficult Conversations with Mind-fulness

Mindful communication becomes especially
valuable in difficult or emotionally charged conversations. In these moments, the principles of
Zen offer tools for maintaining calm, clarity, and
compassion.

One such tool is *nonviolent communication*, a
practice that aligns closely with Zen principles.
Developed by psychologist Marshall Rosenberg,
nonviolent communication involves four steps:
observing the situation without judgment, identifying feelings, expressing needs, and making
requests. This framework encourages dialogue

that is respectful and solution-focused, reducing the likelihood of defensiveness or conflict.

For example, in a disagreement with a colleague, instead of saying, "You always interrupt me," a mindful communicator might say, "I've noticed that during our discussions, I sometimes don't get to finish my thoughts. I feel frustrated because I value being heard. Can we find a way to ensure we both have time to speak?" This approach shifts the focus from blame to collaboration, fostering understanding and cooperation.

The Power of Silence in Communication

In Zen, silence is as important as speech. Far from being an absence, silence creates a space for reflection, understanding, and connection. It allows both the speaker and the listener to process their thoughts and emotions, bringing clarity to the conversation.

The Zen practice of *ma*, or the space between things, applies to communication as well. By allowing moments of silence to exist within a dialogue, we honor the natural rhythm of the conversation, giving both parties time to gather their thoughts and respond thoughtfully.

For instance, in a heated discussion, a brief pause can help diffuse tension and create room for empathy. Similarly, in moments of shared joy or sorrow, silence can convey more than words, expressing a depth of presence and care that transcends language.

Creating a Culture of Mindful Communication

Mindful communication is not only a personal practice but also a way to cultivate harmony in groups and communities. By modeling the principles of mindful communication—listening actively, speaking with intention, and honoring silence—we create an environment where others feel safe and respected.

In family settings, this might involve setting aside time for meaningful conversations, free from distractions like phones or television. In professional settings, it could mean fostering a culture of openness and collaboration, where all voices are valued and heard. These practices strengthen relationships and build a foundation of trust and mutual respect.

The Transformative Potential of Mindful Communication

When practiced consistently, mindful communication transforms not only our relationships but also our own sense of self-awareness and connection. It shifts our focus from reacting to responding, from competing to collaborating, and from speaking to connecting. This transformation fosters a sense of harmony and fulfillment that enriches every aspect of our lives.

Zen master Thích Nhất Hạnh captures this potential beautifully: "Speak the truth, but not to punish. Speak with love so that you can restore communication and understanding." These words remind us that communication is not a tool for asserting power or dominance but a means of fostering understanding and compassion.

Conclusion: A Path to Connection and Harmony

Mindful communication is a practice of presence, intention, and care. By listening deeply, speaking thoughtfully, and embracing silence, we create dialogues that honor both ourselves and others. Zen teaches us that communication is not just about exchanging words but about building bridges—bridges of trust, empathy, and connection.

As we continue to explore the principles of resolving conflict in the next section, the practices of mindful communication provide a foundation for navigating even the most challenging interactions with clarity and grace. Through this journey, we discover that true harmony begins with the simple act of being present with one another.

Resolving Conflict with Mindfulness

Conflict, while often uncomfortable, is a natural part of human relationships. Differences in perspectives, needs, and expectations can lead to misunderstandings and disagreements. Yet, when approached with mindfulness and patience, conflict becomes an opportunity for growth, understanding, and deeper connection. Zen offers profound insights and practical tools for navigating conflict with clarity, compassion, and a calm heart.

Understanding the Nature of Conflict

In Zen, conflict is not viewed as inherently negative but as a reflection of the dynamic and interconnected nature of life. Just as a river flows and bends around obstacles, relationships require flexibility and adaptation. Conflict arises when rigidity takes hold—when we cling to our own viewpoints, resist change, or react impulsively.

The first step in resolving conflict mindfully is to recognize its impermanence. Like all things in life, conflict is transient, a momentary disturbance that can be navigated and transformed. By embracing this perspective, we can approach disagreements with a sense of curiosity and openness, rather than fear or defensiveness.

The Zen Practice of Pausing

One of the most powerful tools for resolving conflict is the practice of pausing. In the heat of a disagreement, emotions can escalate quickly, clouding our judgment and fueling reactive behavior. Zen teaches that by taking a moment to pause, we create space for reflection and intentional action.

This pause might involve taking a deep breath, stepping away from the situation temporarily, or silently repeating a calming mantra. The purpose is not to avoid the conflict but to center ourselves, allowing us to respond with clarity and mindfulness rather than reacting impulsively.

Consider the story of a Zen master who was insulted by a visitor. Instead of reacting, the master simply smiled and said, "Thank you for your words." Later, when asked why he had not defended himself, the master explained, "If someone offers you a gift and you do not accept it, to whom does the gift belong?" This story highlights the power of choosing how we respond, even in challenging situations.

Listening with the Intent to Understand

A common source of conflict is the feeling of not being heard or understood. Zen emphasizes the importance of listening deeply, not with the intent to respond or argue, but with the intent to understand. This practice, known as *mindful listening*, fosters empathy and helps to de-escalate tension.

To practice mindful listening during a conflict, we can focus on the speaker's words, tone, and emotions, setting aside our own judgments and assumptions. By reflecting back what we hear—such as saying, "It sounds like you're feeling frustrated because…"—we validate the other person's experience and create a foundation for mutual understanding.

Mindful listening also involves noticing our internal reactions without letting them take control. For example, if we feel defensive or angry while listening, we can acknowledge these emotions silently, allowing them to pass without interrupting the conversation. This awareness helps us stay present and engaged, even in difficult moments.

Speaking with Compassion and Clarity

Just as listening mindfully is essential for resolving conflict, so too is speaking with compassion and clarity. Zen teaches that our words have the power to heal or harm, and that mindful speech requires both honesty and kindness.

When expressing our own perspective in a conflict, it is helpful to use "I" statements rather than blaming or accusatory language. For instance, instead of saying, "You never listen to me," we might say, "I feel unheard when I try to share my thoughts." This approach shifts the focus from assigning blame to sharing feelings, making it easier for the other person to engage without defensiveness.

Zen also encourages us to speak from a place of calm rather than reactivity. If emotions are running high, it may be wise to take a break and revisit the conversation later, when both parties are better able to communicate effectively. This pause allows us to approach the dialogue with a clear and open mind.

Finding Common Ground

In Zen, the concept of *interbeing* reminds us that we are all interconnected, and that our well-being is tied to the well-being of others. This perspective encourages us to seek common ground during conflicts, focusing on shared values and goals rather than differences.

One way to find common ground is to identify the underlying needs or intentions behind each person's perspective. For example, in a disagreement about household responsibilities, one person may be seeking support while the other values independence. By recognizing these needs, both parties can work together to find a solution that honors their shared commitment to harmony and balance.

Zen also teaches that compromise is not about winning or losing but about creating a resolution that benefits everyone involved. This requires a willingness to let go of rigid positions and to approach the conversation with a spirit of generosity and flexibility.

The Role of Forgiveness in Conflict Resolution

Forgiveness is a central theme in Zen and an essential part of resolving conflict. Holding onto resentment or anger only perpetuates suffering, both for ourselves and others. Forgiveness does not mean condoning harmful behavior but rather releasing the emotional weight of the conflict, allowing us to move forward with peace and clarity.

Zen encourages us to approach forgiveness as a practice, not a one-time event. This practice begins with self-reflection, acknowledging our own role in the conflict and offering ourselves compassion for any mistakes we may have made. From this place of self-understanding, we can extend forgiveness to others, recognizing that we are all imperfect and striving in our own ways.

The Transformative Potential of Conflict

When approached mindfully, conflict has the potential to deepen relationships and foster personal growth. It challenges us to examine our assumptions, expand our perspectives, and strengthen our communication skills. By resolving conflict with patience and clarity, we build trust and resilience, both within ourselves and in our relationships.

Zen master Thích Nhất Hạnh often spoke of

conflict as an opportunity to practice mindfulness and compassion. He wrote, "When we are mindful, deeply in touch with the present moment, our understanding of what is going on deepens, and we begin to be filled with acceptance, joy, peace, and love." This perspective reminds us that even the most difficult conflicts can be a path to greater harmony and connection.

Conclusion: A Path to Harmony

Resolving conflict mindfully requires patience, presence, and a commitment to understanding. By listening deeply, speaking with compassion, and seeking common ground, we transform disagreements into opportunities for growth and connection. Zen teaches us that conflict, when approached with mindfulness, is not an obstacle but a bridge—a way to deepen our relationships and foster harmony.

As we explore the principles of building deep connections in the next section, the tools and practices of mindful conflict resolution provide a foundation for cultivating relationships that are both resilient and fulfilling. Through this journey, we discover that true harmony is not the absence of conflict but the presence of understanding and compassion.

Building Deep Connections

In the quiet rhythm of a Zen practice, relationships are seen not as separate or static entities but as dynamic, living connections that reflect the principles of mindfulness, compassion, and interdependence. Building deep connections with others is a practice in itself—a practice that calls for presence, authenticity, and care. Through the lens of Zen, relationships become more than interactions; they become a shared path to growth, understanding, and harmony.

The Foundation of Deep Connections

At the heart of every meaningful relationship lies a foundation of trust, respect, and mutual understanding. Zen teaches that these qualities are not built through grand gestures or perfect words but through consistent, mindful presence. Just as a garden flourishes with regular attention and care, relationships thrive when we nurture them with intention.

The concept of *sangha* in Zen—meaning a community of practitioners—underscores the importance of relationships in our spiritual and personal journeys. Within a *sangha*, individuals support one another in cultivating mindfulness and compassion, creating a collective energy of understanding and peace. This principle can be extended to all our relationships, reminding us that deep connections arise from a shared commitment to growth and mutual well-being.

The Power of Being Present

Presence is one of the most profound gifts we can offer in any relationship. In Zen, presence is not just about physical proximity but about being fully engaged and attentive in the moment. When we are present with others, we communicate that they are valued, seen, and heard.

Consider the simple act of sharing a meal with a loved one. In a Zen-inspired approach, this is not merely a routine activity but an opportunity to connect deeply. By putting away distractions, savoring each bite, and engaging in mindful conversation, we create a shared experience that fosters closeness and joy. This kind of presence transforms ordinary moments into extraordinary ones, strengthening the bond between us.

The story of Zen master Dogen illustrates this principle beautifully. When asked how to live a meaningful life, Dogen replied, "Sit, walk, and eat with mindfulness." While seemingly simple, this teaching highlights that the quality of our attention defines the quality of our connections. By being fully present in our interactions, we bring depth and authenticity to our relationships.

Authenticity as a Cornerstone

Authenticity is another cornerstone of deep connections. Zen teaches that true connection cannot be forged on pretense or illusion; it requires us to show up as we are, with vulnerability and honesty. This does not mean sharing every thought or emotion indiscriminately but being genuine in our intentions and actions.

In practice, authenticity involves expressing our

needs and boundaries with clarity and kindness, as well as creating space for others to do the same. It means embracing our imperfections and allowing others to see them, trusting that true connection arises not from perfection but from shared humanity.

For example, in a professional setting, a leader who admits their mistakes and seeks input from their team fosters an environment of trust and collaboration. Similarly, in personal relationships, sharing our fears and dreams with a loved one can deepen the bond between us, creating a sense of mutual understanding and support.

The Role of Compassion in Building Connections

Compassion, a central tenet of Zen, is the thread that weaves relationships together. When we approach others with an open heart and a willingness to understand their experiences, we create a space where connection can flourish. Compassion allows us to see beyond surface differences, recognizing the shared struggles and joys that unite us.

One way to practice compassion in relationships is to adopt a mindset of curiosity rather than judgment. When a friend or colleague expresses frustration, for instance, we can choose to explore the underlying emotions rather than reacting defensively. This curiosity fosters empathy and creates an opportunity for meaningful dialogue.

Zen also encourages us to extend compassion to ourselves, recognizing that our ability to connect with others is influenced by how we treat ourselves. By cultivating self-compassion, we build the inner resilience needed to approach relationships with patience and care.

Creating Rituals of Connection

In Zen, rituals are not rigid or formal but intentional practices that bring mindfulness and meaning to daily life. Similarly, creating rituals of connection in our relationships can strengthen bonds and foster a sense of belonging.

These rituals might be as simple as sharing a

cup of tea each morning with a partner, setting aside time for weekly check-ins with a friend, or starting team meetings with a moment of gratitude. By establishing these practices, we create consistent opportunities to connect and reflect, even amid the busyness of life.

One Zen-inspired ritual is the practice of loving-kindness meditation, or *metta*. This involves silently offering wishes of well-being to ourselves and others, such as "May you be happy. May you be healthy. May you live with ease." Practicing *metta* regularly can deepen our sense of connection and compassion, both in existing relationships and in our interactions with strangers.

Navigating Challenges with Grace

Deep connections are not free from challenges; in fact, it is often through navigating difficulties that relationships grow stronger. Zen teaches that challenges are opportunities to practice patience, humility, and forgiveness—qualities that deepen our bonds with others.

When misunderstandings or conflicts arise, approaching them with mindfulness and openness allows us to address issues without damaging the relationship. This might involve acknowledging our own role in the situation, listening deeply to the other person's perspective, and working collaboratively toward a resolution. These practices not only resolve the immediate issue but also build trust and resilience within the relationship.

The Joy of Shared Presence

The ultimate reward of building deep connections is the joy that comes from shared presence — the feeling of being truly seen and accepted by another. In Zen, this joy is not dependent on external circumstances but arises from the quality of the connection itself. Whether sharing a moment of laughter, supporting one another through challenges, or simply sitting in silence together, these experiences remind us of the beauty and richness of human connection.

Thích Nhất Hạnh often spoke of the "peace of togetherness," a state of harmony that arises when individuals are fully present with one another. This peace is not about avoiding conflict or seeking perfection but about embracing the fullness of the relationship, with all its complexities and nuances.

Conclusion: A Practice of Connection

Building deep connections is a lifelong practice, one that requires mindfulness, compassion, and intention. By being present, authentic, and compassionate, we create relationships that are not only meaningful but transformative. Zen teaches us that these connections are both a reflection of our inner state and a source of growth and joy, reminding us of the profound beauty of walking through life together.

As we conclude this chapter, the principles of building deep connections offer a guide for cultivating harmony and fulfillment in all our relationships. They remind us that connection is not something we find but something we create—a practice that enriches both ourselves and the world around us.

CHAPTER 7: ZEN AND CREATIVITY – UNLOCKING THE FLOW STATE

The Connection Between Zen and Creativity

Creativity, in its purest form, is an act of flow — a seamless and intuitive process that bridges thought, emotion, and expression. For centuries, artists, writers, and innovators have sought ways to access this state, a state that Zen naturally cultivates through its principles of mindfulness, detachment, and presence. The connection between Zen and creativity lies in their shared essence: the ability to transcend distractions and engage fully with the moment, allowing inspiration to arise effortlessly.

The Zen Perspective on Creativity

In Zen, creativity is not viewed as a talent or skill reserved for the select few. Instead, it is seen as a natural and universal expression of the human spirit, one that flourishes when the mind is free and present. This perspective aligns with the Zen principle of *shikantaza*, or "just sitting," which encourages practitioners to let go of striving and simply be with their experience. Similarly, creativity often emerges not from force or effort but from a state of relaxed awareness.

Consider the practice of Zen calligraphy, where each brushstroke is a reflection of the practitioner's state of mind. The focus is not on achieving perfection but on expressing the present moment with authenticity and grace. In this way, Zen teaches that creativity is less about the end result and more about the process—a process that becomes meaningful when approached with mindfulness and intention.

Mindfulness as a Gateway to Creativity

Mindfulness, the cornerstone of Zen practice, is a powerful catalyst for creativity. By bringing full attention to the present moment, mindfulness quiets the noise of the mind, making space for fresh ideas and perspectives to emerge. This state of focused awareness allows us to engage deeply with our work, whether it is painting a canvas, composing music, or solving a complex problem.

The poet Matsuo Bashō exemplified this connection between mindfulness and creativity in his haikus, which capture the essence of fleeting moments with clarity and precision. Bashō's ability to distill profound beauty from the ordinary—an old pond, a falling leaf—demonstrates how mindfulness heightens our perception and awakens our creative potential.

In practical terms, mindfulness can be cultivated through simple practices such as deep breathing, meditation, or even pausing to observe the details of our surroundings. These practices not only enhance our focus but also help us access a state of openness and curiosity, both essential for creative work.

Detachment and the Creative Process

Another key principle of Zen that enhances creativity is detachment—not in the sense of disinterest, but in the ability to release attachment to specific outcomes. Creativity often falters under the weight of expectations, whether it is the pressure to produce something exceptional or the fear of failure. Zen teaches that by letting go of these attachments, we free ourselves to explore, experiment, and create with a sense of playfulness and freedom.

This principle is evident in the story of the Zen archer, who practices *kyūdō* (the way of the bow). In *kyūdō*, the archer's goal is not to hit the target but to perform the act of shooting with mindfulness and intention. By detaching from the result, the archer achieves a state of flow, where the act itself becomes the reward. This approach can be applied to any creative endeavor, reminding us that the journey is as important as the destination.

For example, a writer facing a blank page might feel paralyzed by the desire to craft a perfect first sentence. By adopting a Zen mindset, the writer can release this pressure and focus instead on the act of writing itself, allowing the words to flow naturally. This shift in perspective transforms creativity from a task into an exploration, opening the door to unexpected insights and inspiration.

The Role of Stillness in Creativity

Stillness is another profound aspect of Zen that nurtures creativity. In a world filled with constant activity and stimulation, stillness provides a sanctuary where the mind can rest and recharge. It is in these moments of stillness that ideas often surface, like ripples on a calm pond.

Zen meditation, or *zazen*, offers a structured way to access this stillness. By sitting in silence and observing the breath, practitioners create a space where thoughts can arise and settle without judgment or interference. This practice not only enhances mental clarity but also fosters a sense of receptivity, allowing creative insights to emerge naturally.

The composer John Cage, inspired by Zen philosophy, embraced the value of silence and stillness in his work. His groundbreaking piece "4'33"," in which musicians remain silent for four minutes and thirty-three seconds, challenges traditional notions of music and invites listeners to perceive the sounds of the environment as part of the composition. Cage's work exemplifies how stillness can spark innovation and expand our understanding of creativity.

Creativity as a Practice of Presence

Zen teaches that creativity is not a rare or fleet-ing occurrence but a practice—one that thrives when we approach it with consistency and pres-ence. This practice does not require elaborate rituals or specialized tools; it begins with the simple act of showing up and engaging fully with the task at hand.

The painter Hokusai, known for his iconic series "Thirty-Six Views of Mount Fuji," exemplified this practice. Hokusai dedicated his life to ex-ploring the same subject from countless angles, finding endless inspiration in its variations. His work reminds us that creativity is not about seeking new ideas but about seeing familiar ones with fresh eyes—a skill cultivated through mindfulness and presence.

By integrating creative practices into our daily lives, we can develop a deeper connection to our work and ourselves. Whether it is journaling, sketching, or improvising on a musical instru-ment, these practices invite us to enter a state of flow and discover the joy of creation.

Conclusion: A Path to Creative Freedom

The connection between Zen and creativity lies in their shared emphasis on presence, openness, and flow. Through mindfulness, detachment, and stillness, Zen provides tools for unlocking our creative potential and embracing the process of creation with curiosity and joy. It reminds us that creativity is not a destination but a journey—one that unfolds moment by moment, in the quiet spaces where inspiration resides.

As we explore the conditions for entering the flow state in the next section, the principles of Zen offer a guiding light, showing us how to navigate the creative process with grace and intention. Through this journey, we discover that creativity, like Zen itself, is both a practice and a way of being—a path to deeper connection, expression, and fulfillment.

Entering the Flow State

The flow state, often described as being "in the zone," is a state of heightened focus, effortless action, and complete immersion in an activity. It is where creativity flourishes and where the mind and body align seamlessly to achieve extraordinary outcomes. While the flow state might seem elusive, Zen provides a roadmap for entering and sustaining this powerful state through principles of mindfulness, balance, and intentionality.

Understanding the Flow State Through Zen

In Zen, the flow state is not a mystical or rare phenomenon; it is a natural result of being fully present in the moment. This presence, cultivated through practices like *zazen* (seated meditation) and *kinhin* (walking meditation), quiets the distractions of the mind and creates space for a deeper engagement with the task at hand. When we are present, we become attuned to the subtleties of our work, responding intuitively and effortlessly.

Zen philosophy also teaches that flow arises when we let go of attachment to outcomes and immerse ourselves in the process. This principle mirrors the teachings of psychologist Mihály Csíkszentmihályi, who coined the term "flow" and identified it as a state where challenges and skills are perfectly balanced. In Zen terms, this balance reflects the harmony between effort and ease—a dance between focused intention and relaxed awareness.

The Preconditions for Flow

Entering the flow state requires certain conditions that align closely with Zen practices. The first is clear intention, or *motivation*. Whether we are painting, writing, or solving a problem, having a clear purpose helps to focus our attention and energy. Zen emphasizes the importance of setting an intention before beginning any activity, grounding ourselves in the present moment and aligning our actions with our values.

The second condition is the presence of a meaningful challenge. If a task is too easy, it can lead to boredom; if it is too difficult, it can create anxiety. Flow occurs when the task is just challenging enough to engage our skills without overwhelming us. This principle is echoed in Zen teachings, which encourage practitioners to approach challenges with curiosity and a beginner's mind, viewing them as opportunities for growth rather than obstacles.

Another precondition for flow is minimizing distractions. In a world filled with notifications, multitasking, and constant stimulation, creating a focused environment is essential. Zen offers practical tools for cultivating this focus, such as single-tasking and eliminating unnecessary clutter—both mental and physical. By creating a space that supports concentration, we pave the way for the flow state to emerge.

The Role of Ritual in Entering Flow

Rituals play a significant role in preparing the mind and body for flow. In Zen, rituals are simple yet intentional acts that create a sense of structure and mindfulness. These might include lighting a candle, reciting a mantra, or arranging a workspace with care. Such rituals serve as a bridge between the external world and the internal state of focus, signaling to the mind that it is time to engage fully with the task.

Consider the example of a potter beginning their craft. Before touching the clay, they might take a moment to center themselves, breathing deeply and visualizing the piece they wish to create. This act of preparation not only calms the mind but also establishes a sense of purpose and presence, setting the stage for flow.

Rituals can also be incorporated into modern creative practices. A writer might begin their day by journaling or reading a poem, while a musician might tune their instrument mindfully before playing. These small acts of intention help to anchor us in the present moment, creating a fertile ground for inspiration and flow.

The Balance Between Effort and Ease

One of the most profound insights Zen offers about the flow state is the importance of balancing effort and ease. In Zen, this balance is known as *wu wei*, or "effortless action." It does not mean the absence of effort but rather a harmony between purposeful action and natural flow. When we try too hard, we create tension; when we let go too much, we lose focus. The sweet spot lies in cultivating a sense of relaxed concentration.

This balance can be seen in the practice of ar-

chery, a discipline often associated with Zen.
A master archer does not force the bowstring
but allows the arrow to release with precision
and grace, guided by years of practice and a
calm mind. Similarly, in creative endeavors, we
achieve flow by trusting our skills and allowing
the process to unfold naturally, without overthinking or second-guessing.

Staying in the Flow State

Once we enter the flow state, sustaining it requires a delicate interplay of focus, adaptability,
and self-awareness. Zen teaches that distractions are inevitable, but our response to them
determines whether we remain in flow or lose
our rhythm. By gently redirecting our attention
back to the task, much like returning to the
breath during meditation, we can maintain our
connection to the moment.

It is also important to honor the body and mind
during periods of intense focus. Zen emphasizes the value of taking mindful breaks, whether
through stretching, walking, or simply pausing
to breathe. These moments of rest prevent burnout and help to sustain energy and creativity

over longer periods.

Another practice for staying in flow is to embrace imperfection. Zen's principle of *wabi-sabi* celebrates the beauty of the imperfect and the unfinished, reminding us that creativity is a process, not a product. By letting go of the need for perfection, we free ourselves to experiment and take risks, deepening our engagement with the task.

The Joy of Flow

The ultimate reward of the flow state is the joy that comes from being fully immersed in the present moment. In Zen, this joy is known as *satori*—a glimpse of enlightenment or profound realization. While flow is not a permanent state, each moment spent in flow brings us closer to this sense of fulfillment and connection.

Artists and innovators throughout history have described the flow state as a source of their greatest achievements. From the sweeping brushstrokes of a painter to the eloquent prose of a writer, flow transforms the act of creation into a transcendent experience, where time seems to dissolve and the self merges with the work.

Conclusion: Flow as a Practice of Presence

Entering the flow state is both an art and a practice, one that requires mindfulness, intention, and a willingness to let go. Zen offers a timeless guide for unlocking this state, showing us how to align effort and ease, focus and flexibility. By cultivating the conditions for flow, we tap into a wellspring of creativity, discovering the joy and fulfillment that arise from being fully present in the act of creation.

As we explore the techniques for overcoming creative blocks in the next section, the principles of Zen and flow provide a foundation for navigating challenges with grace and resilience. Through this journey, we learn that the flow state is not a destination but a way of being—a dynamic and inspired engagement with the world around us.

Overcoming Creative Blocks

Every creative journey encounters obstacles—

moments when ideas stall, motivation wanes, or self-doubt creeps in. These creative blocks can feel insurmountable, leaving us disconnected from the flow of inspiration. Yet, Zen teaches that such blocks are not barriers to creativity but invitations to pause, reflect, and realign with the present moment. By approaching creative challenges with mindfulness, curiosity, and compassion, we can transform these periods of stagnation into opportunities for growth.

Understanding the Nature of Creative Blocks

In Zen, obstacles are seen as part of the natural ebb and flow of life, much like clouds passing across the sky. They are temporary and often the result of attachment—whether to specific outcomes, fears of judgment, or the pressure to succeed. Recognizing this impermanence is the first step in overcoming creative blocks.

A Zen story illustrates this perspective. A monk approached his master, saying, "My mind is restless, and I cannot meditate." The master replied, "Your mind is like a muddy pond. If you stop stirring it, the mud will settle, and the water will become clear." This metaphor applies to creativity as well. When faced with a block, the key is not to push harder but to create stillness, allowing clarity to emerge.

Embracing the Beginner's Mind

One of the most powerful Zen principles for overcoming creative blocks is *shoshin*, or "beginner's mind." This mindset encourages us to approach our work with openness, curiosity, and a willingness to explore without judgment. By letting go of preconceived notions and expectations, we free ourselves to see possibilities we might have overlooked.

For example, a painter struggling to complete a piece might return to the canvas with fresh eyes, experimenting with new techniques or perspectives. Instead of striving for perfection, they focus on the joy of exploration, rediscovering the creative process as a playful and dynamic experience.

Mindfulness as a Tool for Clarity

Mindfulness is another essential practice for navigating creative blocks. By grounding ourselves in the present moment, we can identify the underlying causes of our resistance—whether it is fear, fatigue, or a lack of direction. This awareness allows us to address the root of the issue rather than becoming overwhelmed by its symptoms.

One practical mindfulness exercise is to take a few moments to sit quietly and observe the sensations, thoughts, and emotions associated with the block. Without judgment, simply acknowledge what arises, allowing it to pass like waves on the shore. This practice helps to release tension and create space for new ideas to emerge.

Zen also emphasizes the importance of connecting with the body as a way to reset the mind. Practices such as walking meditation, yoga, or even a simple stretch can help to release physical and mental tension, restoring focus and energy.

Letting Go of Perfectionism

Perfectionism is a common source of creative blocks, fueled by the fear of making mistakes or producing work that does not meet our own standards. Zen offers a counterpoint to this mindset through the concept of *wabi-sabi*, which celebrates imperfection and impermanence as sources of beauty and authenticity.

A potter practicing *wabi-sabi* might embrace the unique flaws in their work—a crack in the glaze, an uneven edge—as reflections of the human hand and the natural world. Similarly, in our creative endeavors, letting go of the need for perfection allows us to focus on the process rather than the outcome, reducing the pressure that stifles inspiration.

For a writer struggling with a blank page, this might mean allowing themselves to draft freely without judgment, knowing that refinement can come later. By shifting the focus from achieving perfection to simply creating, they break through the paralysis of self-criticism and rediscover the joy of expression.

Reconnecting with Purpose

When creativity feels blocked, it is often helpful to revisit the purpose behind our work. Zen teaches that intention is a powerful motivator, guiding our actions with clarity and meaning. Reflecting on why we create—whether to inspire, connect, or explore—can reignite our passion and provide a sense of direction.

One way to reconnect with purpose is through journaling. Writing about our creative goals, values, and aspirations helps to clarify what truly matters, filtering out distractions and doubts. This practice can also uncover hidden motivations or insights, reigniting the spark of inspiration.

The Role of Rest and Renewal

Zen recognizes the importance of rest in the creative process. Just as the body needs sleep to recharge, the mind requires moments of stillness to process and integrate ideas. When faced with a creative block, stepping away from the work can be a powerful act of renewal.

In Zen, this principle is embodied in the practice of *zazen*. By sitting quietly and observing the breath, practitioners create a space where the mind can rest and recalibrate. This stillness often leads to moments of insight and clarity, as the mind naturally organizes itself in the absence of effort.

For creatives, taking a mindful break might involve spending time in nature, engaging in a different activity, or simply allowing the mind to wander. These pauses are not wasted time but essential parts of the creative cycle, providing the energy and perspective needed to move forward.

Experimenting with New Approaches

Sometimes, overcoming a creative block requires stepping outside of our comfort zones and exploring new methods or mediums. Zen encourages this spirit of experimentation, viewing it as an opportunity to expand our horizons and discover unexpected possibilities.

For example, a musician struggling to compose might experiment with a different instrument or genre, while a designer might seek inspiration from unfamiliar cultures or art forms. These shifts in perspective can break the monotony of routine and spark fresh ideas.

Zen also teaches that mistakes are not failures but opportunities for learning and growth. By embracing a willingness to try—and fail—we cultivate resilience and creativity, transforming obstacles into stepping stones.

The Freedom Found in Acceptance

Ultimately, Zen reminds us that creative blocks are not obstacles to be conquered but experiences to be accepted. By approaching these moments with patience and curiosity, we discover that they are part of the natural rhythm of creativity, offering lessons and insights that deepen our understanding of ourselves and our work.

As the Zen master Shunryu Suzuki wrote, "When you realize that everything is just a wave of your mind, there is nothing to be afraid of." This perspective invites us to see creative blocks not as barriers but as waves—temporary and ever-changing, carrying us toward new possibilities.

Conclusion: From Stagnation to Flow

Overcoming creative blocks is a journey of mindfulness, resilience, and self-discovery. By embracing the principles of Zen—beginner's mind, mindfulness, and acceptance—we transform these challenges into opportunities for growth and renewal. In doing so, we unlock the flow of inspiration and reconnect with the joy of creation.

As we explore the practices for sustaining creative energy in the next section, the tools for overcoming creative blocks provide a foundation for navigating the highs and lows of the creative process with grace and intention. Through this journey, we learn that creativity, like Zen, is a practice—a dynamic and evolving path toward greater expression and fulfillment.

Sustaining Creative Energy

Creativity, like any form of energy, ebbs and flows. Moments of inspiration can feel boundless, but sustaining that energy over time requires balance, mindfulness, and intention. In Zen, the art of maintaining creative vitality mirrors the rhythms of nature, where cycles of growth and rest are essential for renewal. By harmonizing effort with rest and fostering habits that support long-term creativity, we can cultivate a wellspring of energy that nourishes both our work and our well-being.

The Principle of Balance in Zen

Zen emphasizes balance as a cornerstone of a harmonious life. This balance extends to the creative process, where effort must be tempered with rest, and intensity balanced with reflection. When we push too hard, we risk burnout; when we disengage completely, our creative spark can dim. Sustaining creative energy requires navigating this delicate equilibrium with mindfulness and care.

A Zen analogy often used to illustrate this balance is the string of a lute. If the string is too tight, it will snap; if it is too loose, it will not produce sound. The key is to find the right tension—enough to create resonance without strain. Similarly, in creativity, the right balance allows us to work with focus and passion while preserving our energy for the long term.

The Role of Rest and Renewal

Rest is not the opposite of creativity but an integral part of its cycle. In Zen, rest is seen as a form of active engagement—a time to replenish the mind, body, and spirit. Practices like meditation, mindful walking, and simply observing nature provide opportunities to recharge and reconnect with the present moment.

One Zen teaching highlights the importance of pauses: "Do not follow the flow of the river endlessly. Sometimes, stop and sit by its banks to appreciate its beauty." For creatives, this pause might mean stepping away from a project, spending time in a restorative environment, or engaging in activities unrelated to their work. These moments of stillness and renewal often lead to fresh insights and a deeper connection to the creative process.

Building Sustainable Routines

Zen teaches that consistency, rather than intensity, is the foundation of lasting progress. This principle applies to creativity as well. Developing a sustainable routine helps to channel creative energy in a way that is both productive and nourishing. Such routines provide structure without stifling spontaneity, creating a rhythm that supports regular engagement with creative work.

For example, a writer might dedicate a specific time each day to their craft, allowing for both focused effort and moments of rest. Similarly, an artist might alternate between periods of intense creation and quieter times of reflection or experimentation. These routines create a sense of stability, making it easier to return to the work even during periods of low motivation.

Zen also encourages the practice of setting realistic goals—goals that challenge us without overwhelming us. By breaking larger projects into manageable steps, we can maintain momentum and avoid the exhaustion that comes from trying to do too much at once.

Mindfulness and Energy Management

Mindfulness is a powerful tool for sustaining creative energy. By cultivating awareness of our physical, emotional, and mental states, we can recognize when our energy is waning and take steps to restore it. This might involve adjusting our pace, seeking inspiration, or simply pausing to breathe.

One practical application of mindfulness is the practice of body scanning—a technique often used in Zen meditation. By tuning in to the sensations in the body, we can identify areas of tension or fatigue and respond with care. For instance, noticing tight shoulders might prompt a stretch or a break, while feelings of mental fog could signal the need for rest or a change of scenery.

Mindfulness also helps us to stay present with our work, reducing the energy lost to distractions or overthinking. When we focus fully on the task at hand, we enter a state of flow where creativity feels effortless and energizing.

The Importance of Joy and Play

Zen reminds us that creativity is not only about producing results but also about experiencing joy and playfulness in the process. Engaging with our work in a spirit of curiosity and exploration helps to sustain our enthusiasm and prevent creative fatigue.

This principle is evident in the Zen practice of *enso*—the drawing of a circle in one continuous brushstroke. Each *enso* is unique, reflecting the mood and energy of the moment. The practice is not about achieving perfection but about embracing the act of creation with an open heart. Similarly, approaching our creative work with a sense of play allows us to experiment, take risks, and discover new possibilities.

Incorporating elements of play into our routines can take many forms, from trying new techniques to collaborating with others or even revisiting creative activities from childhood. These playful moments rekindle our passion and remind us of the joy that drew us to our craft in the first place.

Nurturing the Creative Environment

The environment in which we create has a profound impact on our energy and focus. Zen encourages us to cultivate spaces that support mindfulness and inspiration—spaces that are uncluttered, intentional, and aligned with our creative goals.

For some, this might mean designing a workspace that is clean and organized, with tools and materials readily accessible. For others, it could involve incorporating elements of nature, such as plants, natural light, or soothing sounds. These small adjustments create an atmosphere that fosters calm and clarity, enhancing our ability to sustain creative energy.

Zen also teaches the value of connecting with the larger environment, whether through spending time outdoors, observing the changing seasons, or engaging with the community. These connections ground us in the present moment and provide fresh perspectives that energize our work.

Celebrating Progress and Reflection

Finally, sustaining creative energy requires acknowledging and celebrating progress, no matter how small. Zen emphasizes the importance of reflection—taking time to appreciate what we have accomplished and to learn from our experiences. This practice not only reinforces our motivation but also deepens our understanding of ourselves and our creative process.

A musician, for example, might listen to recordings of their performances, reflecting on moments of growth and areas for improvement. A writer might reread their work with an eye for themes and insights that have emerged over time. These acts of reflection create a sense of continuity, reminding us that creativity is a journey, not a destination.

Conclusion: The Long Path of Creativity

Sustaining creative energy is a practice of balance, mindfulness, and intention. By harmonizing effort with rest, joy with discipline, and focus with play, we create a foundation for enduring creativity. Zen teaches us that this path is not linear but cyclical, with moments of inspiration and renewal woven together in a dynamic flow.

As we conclude this chapter, the principles of sustaining creative energy offer a guide for navigating the ups and downs of the creative process with grace and resilience. Through this journey, we discover that creativity, like Zen, is a lifelong practice—one that enriches our lives and connects us to the boundless potential of the present moment.

CHAPTER 8: LIVING ZEN – SUSTAINING BALANCE IN A BUSY WORLD

Integrating Zen into Everyday Life

In the Zen tradition, the boundaries between practice and daily life dissolve. Rather than confining mindfulness to the meditation cushion or limiting simplicity to the confines of a Zen garden, the true essence of Zen lies in its integration into the rhythms of everyday life. Zen teaches us that even the most mundane tasks—washing dishes, walking to work, or brewing tea—can become opportunities for mindfulness, presence, and harmony. By weaving Zen into our daily routines, we create a life imbued with intention, balance, and joy.

The Ordinary as Sacred

Zen emphasizes that enlightenment is not found in grand gestures or distant realms but in the simple and ordinary moments of life. This perspective is encapsulated in the Zen saying, "Before enlightenment, chop wood, carry water. After enlightenment, chop wood, carry water." The act of chopping wood or carrying water becomes a practice of presence when performed with full attention and care.

One way to integrate Zen into daily life is to approach routine tasks with mindfulness. Consider the act of cooking a meal. Instead of rushing through the process, we might slow down, paying attention to the texture of the vegetables, the sound of the knife slicing through them, and the aroma as they sizzle in the pan. By being fully present, we transform cooking from a chore into a moment of meditation.

This approach applies to all aspects of life, from folding laundry to writing emails. Each task, no matter how small, becomes an opportunity to practice mindfulness, deepen our awareness, and connect with the present moment.

Creating Rituals of Presence

Rituals play a significant role in integrating Zen into daily life. These are not elaborate or time-consuming ceremonies but simple, intentional acts that anchor us in the here and now. A morning ritual, for instance, might involve sitting quietly with a cup of tea, setting an intention for the day, or practicing a few minutes of deep breathing.

Incorporating Zen rituals into daily routines helps to create a sense of structure and mindfulness. For example, beginning and ending the day with a brief meditation practice can provide a grounding point, allowing us to carry a sense of calm and clarity into the rest of the day. Similarly, taking a few mindful breaths before starting a meeting or transitioning between tasks can create a moment of stillness amidst the busyness.

These rituals serve as reminders to pause, reconnect with ourselves, and approach each moment with intention and presence.

The Art of Single-Tasking

One of the greatest challenges in modern life is the tendency to multitask—checking emails while eating lunch, scrolling through social media during conversations, or juggling multiple responsibilities at once. Zen teaches that multitasking scatters our attention, reducing both the quality of our work and our connection to the present moment.

Single-tasking, or focusing on one task at a time, is a core practice in Zen. By giving our full attention to a single activity, we cultivate a sense of flow and engagement that enhances both our efficiency and our enjoyment. For instance, instead of hurriedly answering emails while distracted by other tasks, we might dedicate a specific time to email responses, approaching them with clarity and focus.

The practice of single-tasking also applies to relationships. When we are fully present with others—listening without distractions, maintaining eye contact, and responding thoughtfully—we deepen our connections and foster greater understanding. This simple shift in attention transforms interactions into meaningful exchanges.

Mindful Movement

Zen recognizes that mindfulness is not limited to stillness; it extends to movement as well. Activities such as walking, gardening, or even sweeping the floor can become opportunities for mindful practice. By bringing awareness to the sensations of the body, the rhythm of our steps, or the sound of the broom on the floor, we ground ourselves in the present moment.

Walking meditation, a traditional Zen practice known as *kinhin*, exemplifies this integration of mindfulness and movement. In *kinhin*, practitioners walk slowly and deliberately, focusing on the sensation of each step and the connection between their body and the earth. This practice can be incorporated into daily routines, whether during a walk in nature, a commute, or a moment of transition between activities.

Mindful movement not only enhances our physical and mental well-being but also reminds us of the interconnectedness between ourselves and the world around us. Each step becomes a reflection of presence, each action an expression of mindfulness.

Simplifying and Decluttering

Another way to integrate Zen into daily life is through the practice of simplicity. Zen teaches that by letting go of unnecessary distractions, possessions, and obligations, we create space for what truly matters. This principle can be applied to both our physical spaces and our mental landscapes.

In our homes, this might involve decluttering and organizing to create a calming and functional environment. A clean and uncluttered space reflects the Zen aesthetic of simplicity, promoting a sense of peace and clarity. Similarly, simplifying our schedules—prioritizing meaningful activities and saying no to unnecessary commitments—helps to reduce stress and maintain balance.

Mentally, we can practice simplicity by letting go of negative thought patterns, unproductive habits, and the need for constant stimulation. Meditation, journaling, or simply taking a moment to pause and breathe can help to quiet the mind and refocus our energy on what is truly important.

Integrating Zen into Relationships

Zen is not only a personal practice but also a relational one. By bringing mindfulness, compassion, and authenticity into our interactions, we cultivate harmony and connection with others. This might involve practicing active listening, expressing gratitude, or approaching conflicts with patience and understanding.

In family or community settings, shared Zen-inspired practices—such as cooking together, meditating as a group, or simply enjoying moments of silence—can strengthen bonds and create a sense of shared presence. These practices remind us that Zen is not about retreating from the world but engaging with it fully and mindfully.

The Ripple Effect of Everyday Zen

As we integrate Zen into our daily lives, its impact extends beyond ourselves. Our presence and mindfulness create a ripple effect, influencing our relationships, work, and environment in positive ways. A calm and centered individual inspires calm and clarity in others, fostering a collective sense of harmony and balance.

Zen master Thích Nhất Hạnh often spoke of "engaged mindfulness," the practice of bringing Zen into every aspect of life, from personal actions to social interactions. This engagement transforms not only our inner world but also the world around us, creating a more mindful and compassionate society.

Conclusion: A Practice for Life

Integrating Zen into everyday life is not a destination but an ongoing practice—a way of being that transforms the ordinary into the extraordinary. By approaching daily routines with mindfulness, simplicity, and intention, we create a life that reflects the essence of Zen: balance, presence, and joy.

As we explore the principles of maintaining balance amidst chaos in the next section, the strategies for integrating Zen into daily life provide a foundation for navigating the complexities of the modern world with grace and resilience. Through this journey, we discover that Zen is not something we do; it is something we live—a practice that enriches every moment, every action, and every connection.

Maintaining Balance Amidst Chaos

The world is in constant motion—filled with demands, distractions, and unpredictability. In such a dynamic environment, maintaining balance can feel like walking a tightrope. Yet, Zen offers timeless wisdom for staying grounded and centered amidst chaos. By cultivating presence, practicing simplicity, and embracing flexibility, we can navigate life's turbulence with grace and resilience, transforming chaos into a dance of harmony.

The Still Point Within

Zen teaches that amidst the whirlwind of activity, there exists a still point—a calm center that remains untouched by external noise. This stillness is not about escaping the chaos but about finding stability within it. Through mindfulness practices, we learn to anchor ourselves in this inner stillness, accessing a wellspring of clarity and peace.

Consider the metaphor of a tree in a storm. While its branches may sway and its leaves flutter, its roots remain firmly grounded. Similarly, by cultivating mindfulness, we root ourselves in the present moment, allowing us to weather life's storms without being uprooted.

One simple practice for connecting with this stillness is mindful breathing. In moments of stress or overwhelm, pausing to take a few deep breaths can help to reset the nervous system and restore a sense of balance. By focusing on the inhale and exhale, we bring our attention back to the present, creating a moment of calm amidst the chaos.

Letting Go of the Illusion of Control

A significant source of imbalance in a busy world is the struggle to control the uncontrollable. Zen teaches that much of life is beyond our grasp, and true balance comes from embracing this reality with equanimity. By letting go of the illusion of control, we free ourselves from unnecessary stress and open ourselves to the flow of life.

This principle is beautifully illustrated in the story of a Zen master and a farmer. When the farmer's horse ran away, his neighbors exclaimed, "What bad luck!" The farmer replied, "Maybe." When the horse returned with a group of wild horses, the neighbors said, "What good fortune!" Again, the farmer replied, "Maybe." Through this detachment, the farmer remained balanced, unaffected by the fluctuations of circumstance.

In our own lives, practicing acceptance can help us maintain balance amidst uncertainty. This does not mean resignation but rather a willingness to adapt and respond with flexibility. When a meeting is canceled, a project delayed, or plans disrupted, we can choose to see these moments not as obstacles but as opportunities for growth and reflection.

Creating Space for Rest and Reflection

In a culture that prizes productivity, rest is often undervalued. Yet, Zen recognizes that rest is not a luxury but a necessity for maintaining balance. Just as the body needs sleep to recover, the mind requires moments of stillness to process and rejuvenate.

Incorporating mindful breaks into a busy schedule can be transformative. These breaks might involve a short walk, a few minutes of silent meditation, or simply stepping away from screens to gaze out the window. By creating space for rest and reflection, we prevent burnout and cultivate the energy needed to engage fully with our responsibilities.

Zen master Thích Nhất Hạnh often spoke of the power of *stopping*. He wrote, "Sometimes we need to stop everything we are doing and rest, to bring our mind home to our body, to reconnect with ourselves." This practice of stopping allows us to step out of the rush and reconnect with what truly matters, restoring our sense of balance and purpose.

Simplifying to Create Clarity

Another key to maintaining balance is simplifying our lives. Zen teaches that complexity and clutter—whether physical, mental, or emotional—can weigh us down, making it harder to stay centered. By letting go of what no longer serves us, we create space for clarity and focus.

This might involve decluttering our physical

environment, streamlining our commitments, or prioritizing the tasks and relationships that align with our values. For instance, a professional overwhelmed by back-to-back meetings might reassess their schedule, delegating or rescheduling tasks to create breathing room. Similarly, a parent juggling multiple responsibilities might set boundaries to ensure time for self-care and family connection.

Simplification is not about doing less but about doing what matters most with intention and presence. By focusing on what truly adds value to our lives, we reduce stress and cultivate a sense of balance that sustains us.

Embracing Impermanence and Change

In Zen, impermanence is not something to fear but a natural and beautiful aspect of life. By accepting the transient nature of all things, we learn to navigate change with grace and resilience. This perspective helps us remain grounded even when the world around us feels chaotic.

When faced with a significant change—a career transition, a move, or a shift in relationships—

Zen encourages us to approach it with a beginner's mind. This mindset invites curiosity and openness, allowing us to see new possibilities and adapt to new circumstances without clinging to the past.

For example, someone adjusting to a new job might focus on the opportunity to learn and grow rather than dwelling on what they left behind. Similarly, a family adapting to a new routine might find joy in creating fresh traditions that reflect their current stage of life.

Connecting with Nature

Nature is one of the most powerful allies in maintaining balance. Zen often draws inspiration from the natural world, seeing it as a reflection of harmony and impermanence. Spending time outdoors—whether walking in a park, sitting by a river, or simply observing the sky—grounds us in the present moment and reminds us of our connection to something greater than ourselves.

Incorporating nature into daily life can be as simple as taking a moment to feel the sunlight on your skin, listening to birdsong, or tending to a garden. These small acts of mindfulness bring a sense of calm and perspective, helping us to navigate the busyness of life with greater ease.

The Power of Community

Finally, Zen recognizes the importance of community in maintaining balance. Whether it is a *sangha* (a group of Zen practitioners) or a circle of friends and family, having a supportive community helps us stay grounded and connected.

Sharing experiences, seeking guidance, or simply spending time with others who share our values creates a sense of belonging and mutual support. These connections remind us that we are not alone in our struggles and that balance is a journey best traveled together.

Conclusion: A Dynamic Practice

Maintaining balance amidst chaos is not about achieving a static state but about embracing the dynamic and ever-changing nature of life. Zen teaches us to find stability not in controlling the world around us but in cultivating presence, simplicity, and resilience within ourselves.

As we explore the principles of staying connected to Zen practice in the next section, the tools for maintaining balance provide a foundation for navigating life's complexities with grace and intention. Through this journey, we discover that balance is not a destination but a way of being—a practice that sustains us in the face of life's challenges and joys.

Staying Connected to Your Zen Practice

In the midst of life's busyness, sustaining a commitment to Zen practice can be both challenging and deeply rewarding. Like any meaningful pursuit, Zen requires consistency, intention, and adaptability to flourish over time. Staying connected to your Zen practice is not about rigid adherence but about cultivating a relationship with mindfulness and presence that evolves with your life. By integrating rituals, nurturing motivation, and finding inspiration in both personal and shared experiences, you can deepen your commitment to Zen and keep its wisdom alive in your daily journey.

The Importance of Ritual in Connection

Zen thrives on ritual—not as a set of dogmatic rules but as a series of intentional acts that anchor us to the present moment. These rituals, whether small or elaborate, serve as touchstones that remind us of our commitment to mindfulness and the values we wish to embody.

For example, a morning meditation practice can become a sacred space in your day, a time to center yourself before engaging with the world. Lighting a candle, chanting a mantra, or sipping tea mindfully can transform ordinary actions into moments of presence. Over time, these rituals become habits that ground you, providing a steady rhythm amidst life's unpredictability.

Zen master Shunryu Suzuki emphasized the power of repetition, writing, "When you do something, you should do it with your whole body and mind; you should be concentrated on what you do. You should do it completely, like a good bonfire." In practice, this means approaching each ritual with full attention and intention, allowing even the simplest actions to become profound expressions of your Zen journey.

Finding Motivation Through Reflection

Sustaining a Zen practice often involves revisiting the reasons you were drawn to it in the first place. Reflecting on the impact Zen has had on your life—whether through greater clarity, reduced stress, or a deeper sense of connection—can reignite your motivation and reinforce your commitment.

One powerful tool for reflection is journaling. Taking a few minutes each day or week to write about your experiences with Zen can help you recognize patterns, celebrate progress, and identify areas for growth. You might reflect on questions such as: What moments of mindfulness stood out this week? How has my practice influenced my interactions or decisions? What challenges have I faced, and what have I learned from them?

Reflection not only strengthens your connection to Zen but also deepens your understanding of yourself. It reminds you that Zen is not a static

goal but an evolving practice—one that grows
and changes as you do.

Adapting to Life's Seasons

Life is ever-changing, and so too is your Zen
practice. What works during one season of life
may need to shift in another. Zen teaches the importance of adaptability, encouraging us to flow
with life's currents rather than resisting them.

For example, during particularly busy periods,
your practice might consist of brief moments of
mindfulness—a few conscious breaths, a mindful walk, or a silent pause before a meal. In
quieter times, you might dedicate more time
to meditation, study, or retreats. The key is to
approach these changes with flexibility and
compassion, understanding that Zen is a living
practice that meets you where you are.

This adaptability is reflected in the Zen principle of *mujo*, or impermanence. By embracing
change as a natural part of life, you can sustain your practice without judgment or rigidity,
finding ways to integrate Zen into whatever

circumstances arise.

Seeking Inspiration from Community

While Zen is often seen as an individual journey, community plays a vital role in sustaining your practice. Being part of a *sangha*—a group of fellow practitioners—provides support, encouragement, and accountability. Whether through in-person gatherings, online forums, or shared rituals with loved ones, connecting with others who share your values helps to keep your practice alive and dynamic.

In a *sangha*, the collective energy of the group often amplifies individual commitment. Meditating alongside others, discussing Zen teachings, or simply sharing experiences can deepen your understanding and reignite your enthusiasm. Even when practicing alone, knowing you are part of a larger community can provide a sense of belonging and purpose.

Zen teacher Thích Nhất Hạnh frequently emphasized the importance of community, writing, "The next Buddha may take the form of a community, a community practicing understanding and loving-kindness." This perspective reminds us that Zen is not only about personal growth but also about fostering connection and compassion in the world around us.

Drawing Inspiration from Nature and Teachings

Nature has long been a source of inspiration in Zen, offering endless lessons in impermanence, balance, and interconnectedness. Spending time outdoors—whether observing the changing seasons, walking in the woods, or simply tending to a garden—can rekindle your connection to Zen and remind you of its timeless wisdom.

In addition to nature, Zen teachings and literature provide a rich wellspring of motivation. Reading the words of Zen masters, exploring koans (paradoxical riddles), or studying the principles of mindfulness can deepen your understanding and offer fresh perspectives on your practice. Even revisiting familiar teachings can reveal new insights, as your experiences and interpretations evolve over time.

Celebrating Progress Without Attachment

In Zen, progress is not measured by milestones or achievements but by the quality of your presence and intention. While it is important to acknowledge and celebrate your growth, it is equally important to avoid becoming attached to specific outcomes. Zen teaches that true practice lies in the journey, not the destination.

Celebrating progress might involve acknowledging moments of clarity, expressing gratitude for the benefits of your practice, or simply recognizing the effort you have invested. These small celebrations reinforce your commitment while keeping your focus on the present rather than the end result.

Conclusion: A Lifelong Commitment

Staying connected to your Zen practice is not about perfection but about persistence—a willingness to return to the path again and again, no matter how many times you stray. Through rituals, reflection, adaptability, community, and inspiration, you create a practice that evolves with you, enriching your life in profound and lasting ways.

As we explore the long-term rewards of Zen in the next section, the strategies for staying connected provide a foundation for cultivating a practice that is not only sustainable but trans-formative. Through this journey, you discover that Zen is not a fleeting endeavor but a lifelong companion—a source of balance, wisdom, and joy that supports you through all of life's seasons.

The Long-Term Rewards of Zen

The practice of Zen, though rooted in the simplicity of the present moment, offers profound rewards that unfold over time. These benefits extend far beyond moments of stillness or mindfulness, shaping how we navigate life's challenges, connect with others, and experience the world around us. A Zen-inspired life is not defined by fleeting accomplishments or external validation but by the enduring transformation it brings—one that deepens with each breath, each action, and each day of mindful living.

The Gift of Inner Peace

One of the most immediate and enduring rewards of Zen is inner peace. This peace does not come from the absence of challenges but from the ability to face them with equanimity and clarity. Over time, Zen practice quiets the mental chatter that often fuels anxiety, replacing it with a calm and focused awareness.

Consider the story of a Zen master who, when asked about the secret to happiness, replied, "I see each moment as it is, without wanting it to be otherwise." This perspective, cultivated through years of mindfulness, reflects the profound serenity that arises from acceptance. In daily life, this inner peace manifests as a steadying force, allowing us to remain centered amidst both triumphs and trials.

For example, a busy professional might find that their Zen practice helps them approach deadlines with greater focus and less stress, while a parent might discover a newfound patience in navigating the ups and downs of family life.

This peace is not passive but active—a dynamic state of balance that empowers us to engage with the world fully and authentically.

Strengthening Resilience

Zen teaches that life is inherently unpredictable, marked by cycles of joy and sorrow, gain and loss. By embracing impermanence and letting go of attachment to specific outcomes, we build resilience—the ability to adapt, recover, and grow through life's changes.

Over time, this resilience becomes a cornerstone of a Zen-inspired life. We learn to view setbacks not as failures but as opportunities for growth, approaching challenges with curiosity and courage. This mindset is reflected in the Zen saying, "Fall seven times, stand up eight." It is not about avoiding difficulties but about rising with each fall, fortified by the lessons we have learned.

In practical terms, this resilience might help someone navigate a career transition, cope with the loss of a loved one, or rebuild after a personal setback. By grounding ourselves in the present moment and trusting in our ability to adapt, we discover a wellspring of strength that sustains us through all of life's seasons.

Deepening Relationships

Another long-term reward of Zen is the transformation it brings to our relationships. By cultivating mindfulness, compassion, and presence, we become better equipped to connect with others in meaningful and authentic ways. This shift enhances not only our personal relationships but also our interactions in professional and community settings.

Over time, the practice of mindful communication—listening with full attention, speaking with intention, and responding with empathy—creates a foundation of trust and understanding. This can strengthen bonds with loved ones, improve teamwork and collaboration, and foster a sense of belonging.

Moreover, the Zen principle of *interbeing*—the recognition that all things are interconnected—deepens our appreciation for the relationships that enrich our lives. We come to see each interaction as an opportunity to practice kindness, gratitude, and compassion, creating ripples of positivity that extend far beyond ourselves.

Fostering Creativity and Purpose

Zen also nurtures creativity and purpose, allowing us to engage with our passions and pursuits in a way that is both inspired and sustainable. By quieting the noise of self-doubt and perfectionism, Zen creates space for innovation and exploration, helping us tap into the flow state where ideas flourish.

Over time, this creative energy becomes a source of fulfillment and joy. Whether expressed through art, problem-solving, or acts of service, it reflects our unique contributions to the world. Zen reminds us that purpose is not about grand achievements but about living in alignment with our values and passions, finding meaning in the journey rather than the destination.

For example, an artist might find that their Zen practice helps them approach their work with greater focus and authenticity, while an entrepreneur might discover that mindfulness enhances their decision-making and vision. In both cases, the rewards of Zen extend beyond the individual, inspiring and uplifting those around them.

Living with Gratitude and Joy

As Zen becomes woven into the fabric of daily life, it fosters a profound sense of gratitude and joy. This joy is not tied to external circumstances but arises from the simple act of being present— of savoring the taste of a meal, the warmth of the sun, or the sound of a loved one's laughter.

Gratitude, too, becomes a natural extension of mindfulness. By noticing and appreciating the small blessings that often go unnoticed, we cultivate a sense of abundance and contentment. This shift in perspective transforms how we experience the world, replacing feelings of scarcity or dissatisfaction with a deep appreciation for what is.

Over time, these practices of gratitude and joy create a positive feedback loop, enhancing our well-being and strengthening our connection to life. They remind us that happiness is not something to be pursued but something to be practiced—an ongoing choice to find beauty and meaning in the present moment.

Creating a Legacy of Presence

Perhaps the most profound reward of a Zen-inspired life is the legacy it leaves—not in material terms but in the impact it has on others. By embodying mindfulness, compassion, and balance, we inspire those around us to do the same, creating a ripple effect that extends far beyond our own lives.

This legacy is reflected in the lives of Zen masters whose teachings continue to guide and uplift generations. Yet it is also present in the quiet acts of kindness and presence that define our daily interactions. Each moment of mindfulness, each gesture of compassion, contributes to a world that is more peaceful, connected, and harmonious.

Conclusion: A Life Well Lived

The long-term rewards of Zen are not about achieving a particular state or reaching a final destination. Instead, they are about the ongoing process of living with intention, awareness, and grace. Over time, this practice transforms how we experience life, deepening our sense of peace, resilience, and connection.

As we conclude this chapter, the principles of Zen remind us that these rewards are available to all who commit to the practice—not as something to strive for, but as something to discover in each moment. Through this journey, we come to see that a Zen-inspired life is not only fulfilling but also profoundly liberating—a life rooted in balance, guided by purpose, and enriched by the boundless possibilities of the present.

CONCLUSION: EMBRACING A ZEN-INSPIRED LIFE

As you turn the final pages of this journey into the heart of Zen, take a moment to pause and reflect. The teachings, stories, and practices we have explored together are not distant philosophies or unattainable ideals—they are an invitation to live with greater presence, balance, and intention. Zen offers no final answers, no rigid doctrines, but a path—a way of being that unfolds moment by moment, shaped by your choices and experiences.

This book began with an exploration of Zen's essence: simplicity and harmony. From its roots in ancient philosophy to its relevance in the modern world, Zen has shown us that profound truths can be found in the most ordinary moments. In understanding its principles and practices, we are reminded that the answers we seek often lie not in doing more but in being more—more mindful, more compassionate, more present.

A Life of Simplicity and Presence

At its core, Zen teaches us to embrace simplicity. This is not merely about decluttering our physical spaces but about clearing the mental and emotional clutter that often clouds our lives. By letting go of unnecessary distractions, attachments, and expectations, we create space for what truly matters: the people we cherish, the goals that inspire us, and the beauty of the present moment.

Through mindfulness, we learn to see life as it is, unfiltered by judgment or anxiety. This presence transforms the ordinary into the extraordinary—each breath, each step, each interaction becomes an opportunity to practice Zen. Whether you are preparing a meal, engaging in a conversation, or simply sitting in stillness, mindfulness invites you to experience life fully and authentically.

Resilience Amid Change and Chaos

Zen does not promise a life free from challenges.

Instead, it offers tools to navigate life's inevitable ups and downs with grace and resilience. By embracing impermanence, we learn to see change not as a threat but as a natural part of existence. The art of letting go—whether of material possessions, rigid expectations, or past hurts—frees us to move forward with clarity and courage.

In a world often defined by chaos and busyness, Zen reminds us that balance is possible. Through practices such as meditation, mindful movement, and conscious breathing, we cultivate an inner stillness that anchors us amidst life's turbulence. This stillness is not a retreat but a foundation—a place from which we can engage with the world more effectively and compassionately.

Connections That Nurture and Inspire

No life exists in isolation, and Zen recognizes the profound importance of relationships. By bringing mindfulness and compassion into our interactions, we strengthen our bonds with others and create a ripple effect of kindness and understanding. Whether through active listening, resolving conflicts with patience, or simply being present for a loved one, Zen teaches us to approach relationships with intention and care.

These connections, in turn, nurture us. They remind us of our shared humanity, our inter-connectedness, and the support that is always available when we seek it. As Zen master Thích Nhất Hạnh observed, "Compassion is a verb." It is through our actions—small and large—that we bring the principles of Zen to life, enriching both our own lives and the lives of those around us.

Creativity and Flow in Everyday Life

Zen has much to offer those who seek inspiration and creativity. By quieting the noise of self-doubt and perfectionism, Zen allows us to tap into a deeper source of creativity—one that is natural, effortless, and authentic. The flow state, often described as a hallmark of peak creative experiences, is closely aligned with Zen's emphasis on presence and detachment.

Whether you are an artist, an entrepreneur, or simply someone seeking to approach life with greater imagination, Zen provides tools for unlocking your creative potential. It teaches us to view obstacles as opportunities, to embrace imperfection, and to find joy in the process rather than fixating on the outcome. In doing so, it opens the door to a life that is not only productive but also deeply fulfilling.

A Practice for All Seasons

One of Zen's most profound gifts is its adaptability. Regardless of your circumstances, your stage of life, or your personal challenges, Zen offers practices that meet you where you are. During busy times, a few mindful breaths can bring calm; during quieter moments, meditation or reflection can deepen your understanding. The beauty of Zen lies in its flexibility—it is a practice that evolves with you, offering support and guidance at every turn.

This adaptability is particularly important in a world that often feels overwhelming. By incorporating Zen into your daily routines—through rituals, mindfulness, and acts of kindness—you create a foundation of balance and resilience that sustains you through life's changes. Zen becomes not something you do, but something you live — a way of being that informs your actions, decisions, and relationships.

The Transformative Power of Zen

Over time, the rewards of Zen extend far beyond the individual. As you cultivate inner peace, resilience, and presence, these qualities naturally ripple outward, influencing your relationships, your work, and your community. A Zen-inspired life is not only about personal fulfillment but also about contributing to a more mindful, compassionate world.

This transformation is both subtle and profound. It is reflected in the calm you bring to stressful situations, the patience you show in challenging moments, and the joy you find in simple pleasures. It is evident in the way you approach setbacks, celebrate successes, and navigate the complexities of modern life with grace and intention.

An Invitation to Begin Again

As you close this book, remember that Zen is

not about achieving perfection or adhering to rigid rules. It is about beginning again, each moment, with curiosity and openness. Whether you have been practicing Zen for years or are just starting to explore its principles, each day offers a new opportunity to learn, grow, and live more mindfully.

This journey is not a destination but a practice—a dynamic, evolving process that enriches every aspect of your life. By embracing Zen, you are not only transforming your own experience but also contributing to a world that values presence, compassion, and balance.

A Final Word of Encouragement

Zen reminds us that the present moment is always enough. You do not need to wait for the perfect conditions, the right time, or the absence of challenges to begin living a Zen-inspired life. The tools, insights, and practices shared in this book are yours to explore, adapt, and make your own.

As you step forward, carry with you the lessons of simplicity, mindfulness, and connection. Let them guide your actions, inform your choices, and inspire your journey. And above all, trust in your ability to live with balance and intention, knowing that each moment holds the potential for peace, joy, and transformation.

In the words of Zen master Dogen, "A Zen life is one that is fully lived." May your journey into Zen be one of discovery, growth, and fulfillment—a journey that enriches not only your own life but also the lives of all you touch.

ACKNOWLEDGEMENT

With immense gratitude, I acknowledge the many individuals and inspirations that made this book possible. To my readers, thank you for embarking on this journey of mindfulness and balance. Your curiosity and commitment to growth are the heart of this work.

I extend my deepest appreciation to the Zen masters and philosophers whose timeless teachings have guided not only this book but also my own life. Their wisdom continues to illuminate the path for countless seekers.

To my family and friends, your unwavering support and encouragement have been a steady source of strength. Thank you for your patience and understanding during the countless hours spent immersed in writing.

A special thank you to my collaborators, editors, and creative partners who brought clarity and coherence to these pages. Your insights and dedication have enriched this book immeasurably.

Finally, to the quiet moments of stillness and the everyday experiences that inspired these reflections—thank you for reminding me that the profound often lies in the simple.

This book is a testament to the power of connection, presence, and the enduring beauty of the Zen way. Thank you all for being a part of it.

ABOUT THE AUTHOR

 Felix Grayson's journey into timeless wisdom began in childhood, captivated by the stories of philosophers, leaders, and visionaries who shaped the way we think and live. Growing up in a home filled with books, he spent countless hours exploring ideas that asked life's biggest questions—a curiosity that would later define his work.

After facing his own modern challenges—balancing ambition, uncertainty, and the search for meaning—Felix discovered that the wisdom of the past offers profound guidance for the present. This realization became the foundation for the *Stoned Philosopher* series: a collection dedicated to translating ancient insights into practical lessons for today's world.

Felix's writing is more than reflection—it's an invitation to dialogue with history's greatest minds. Through each book, he helps readers find clarity, resilience, and purpose in their own lives—one timeless idea at a time.

When not writing, Felix enjoys quiet contemplation, deep conversation, and exploring the endless pursuit of wisdom in everyday moments.